"The Hall"
Celebrating the History and Heritage of the United States Hockey Hall of Fame

CLASS OF 2001

"The Hall"
Celebrating the History and Heritage of the U.S. Hockey Hall of Fame
(Class of 2001)

by Ross Bernstein
(www.bernsteinbooks.com)

*All proceeds from the sale of this book go towards the advancement and benefit of the U.S. Hockey Hall of Fame.

To order additional copies of this book, please call the Hall at: (800) 443-7825, or visit their web-site at: www.ushockeyhall.com.

ISBN: 0-9634871-3-2

Cover art by Tim Cortes

Photos courtesy of the Hockey Hall of Fame and the Donald Clark Collection

Printed in the U.S. by Printing Enterprises, New Brighton, MN • (651) 636-9336

Copyright 2001, by Ross Bernstein and the U.S. Hockey Hall of Fame. All rights reserved. This book is not a publication of the NHL or NCAA, and carries along with it no explicit or implied endorsement. The content of this book is the sole responsibility of the U.S. Hockey Hall of Fame.

(*Some of the contents of this book were updated and transcribed from the previous inductee pamphlet which was done by the Hall in 1982)

Acknowledgements:
We would like to thank the following for helping to make this project possible:
Tim Cortes
Jim Findley
Tom Sersha
Michelle Putzel
Paulette Pfremmer
Bonnie Vincent
Dean Vincent
Kathy Trach
Ben Squires
Shari Aubol
Pat Forciea
Amy Woog Patnode
Lee Reed
Tim Trainor
Roger Godin
Don & Tom Clark

COVER ART BY TIM CORTES

One of the nation's premier photo realism artists, Tim Cortes uses colored pencils as his preferred medium. Hundreds of his collectible lithographs have been sold throughout North America and his clients are a venerable who's-who of the American sports world. From Shaquille O'Neal to Mark McGwire and from Wayne Gretzky to Troy Aikman, Cortes has been commissioned to create countless commemorative works of art over the past decade.

His paintings have also been featured in numerous venues around the world as well, including: the US Hockey Hall of Fame, Franklin Mint, Kelly Russell Studios and Beckett's Magazine, as well as on trading cards, pro sports teams' game-day programs, and in various publications. Known for his impeccable detail, Cortes has dedicated his life to the pursuit of celebrating the life and times of many of the world's most famous athletes and the sporting events in which they play.

Cortes grew up in Duluth, where he later starred as a hockey goaltender at Duluth East High School. After a brief stint in the United States Hockey League, Cortes went on to play between the pipes for two seasons in the mid-1980s for the University of Minnesota's Golden Gophers. Cortes then decided to pursue his passion of art and sports full-time, and enrolled at the prestigious Minneapolis College of Art and Design.

Today Tim lives in Duluth with his wife Kathy and their two children. He continues to play Senior-A hockey, and also gives back by coaching both youth hockey and football.

If you would like to purchase a signed, limited edition print of the cover paintings, *"Squaw Valley Gold"* or *"The Class of 2000"* — last year's cover painting, as well as any other of his hundreds of works of art, please check out Tim's web-site or contact his new studio in Duluth, where you, too, can own a wonderful piece of sports history.

Tim Cortes Studio
Original Sports Art

921 North 40th Ave. East
Duluth, MN 55804
(218) 525-4953

WWW.TIMCORTESART.COM

INTRODUCTION

Cooperstown, Canton and Springfield... all small, quaint towns that have one thing in common — they are the homes to America's premier sports Halls of Fames. Why, you might ask, are they located in "out of the way" locales? Simple. Because that is where those respective sports' histories all began. Abner Doubleday first played his new game of baseball in the tiny up-state New York town of Cooperstown, Dr. James Naismith invented the game of basketball in Springfield, Mass., and the NFL was founded just outside of Canton, Ohio, by several men, including the great Jim Thorpe.

Where am I going with all of this? To surely answer the question as to why the United States Hockey Hall of Fame (USHHF) is located in the sleepy Northern Minnesota town of Eveleth. As Minnesotans, we are very proud of our hockey heritage. Like basketball is to Indiana and football to Texas, so too is the ice game revered in the Land of 10,000 Lakes. Simply put, Eveleth is synonymous with American hockey.

Hockey first came to Minnesota via the late James J. Hill's railroad, down through the northwestern corner of the state, near the towns of Roseau and Warroad. It came here due to the fact that at the time, there wasn't a trans-continental rail-line connecting the far western and far eastern borders of Canada. As a result, the trains came down through Minnesota, over to Chicago and Detroit, and on up north of the border. Soon, the teams scheduled stops, and the with it, hockey quickly took off.

Meanwhile, while the modern game of hockey was being perfected in Canada in the mid-1800s, it finally came to the United States in the late 1880s, both along the East Coast and also in Minnesota. It didn't get to Eveleth, however, until around the turn of the century, when the wealthy iron mine owners decided that this new ice game might be a fun form of entertainment to keep their workers happy during those long winters. With that, the city imported a group of top-notch Canadian players and formed a semi-pro team called the Reds, which played a big-time schedule in the USAHA against teams from as far away as New York, Boston, Pittsburgh Chicago and Detroit.

The multi-ethnic miners soon took to the ice game, and it quickly became the common bond that held the community together. Kids became obsessed with the sport, and it became entrenched in the community. Before long, Eveleth was producing the nation's top talent at the high school, amateur, collegiate, semi-pro and professional ranks, with a new crop of kids coming up every year to pass the torch.

Kids like John Mariucci, Frank Brimsek and Mike Karakas were the idols of the next generation of stars which included the likes of John Mayasich, Willard Ikola, Wally Grant and John Matchefts. It just kept growing and growing, until the town was completely obsessed with the game of hockey.

From those humble beginnings, it only seemed appropriate that the community which gave so much to the development and advancement of the game of hockey, be so honored to serve as the host city for our Hall of Fame. That's what this book is all about, celebrating and honoring the history and heroes of American hockey, while promoting the game which has brought so much joy to all of our lives. Enjoy!

A LETTER FROM THE PRESIDENT

Welcome to the second annual publication of "The Hall," a commemorative book honoring the enshrinees and award recipients of the U.S. Hockey Hall of Fame.

The U.S. Hockey Hall of Fame was started in 1967 by the Project H Committee from the Eveleth Civic Association. Through their efforts and commitment, the Hall was opened in 1973 in Eveleth, Minn., the "Capital of American Hockey." The mission of the Hall is to honor those Americans who have made significant contributions to the game of hockey at all levels as players, coaches, referees builders, and administrators. Each year a class of enshrinees have been added to the membership. Including the class of 2001, 110 honorees have been enshrined.

I hope you, as a hockey fan, enjoy reading about the people who have developed our great game and I invite you to visit the Hall to enjoy all the new and updated displays and artifacts. New additions such as the Wall of Fame, the Olympic displays of our 1960, 1980, and 1998 Gold Medal teams, and the scoreboard used in the Mighty Ducks movie are all there for everyone to enjoy. And, as we approach the 2002 Winter Olympic Games in Salt Lake City, additional exhibits honoring the men's and women's teams will be added as well.

Our Executive Director, Tom Sersha, continues to improve and add exhibits at the Hall on a regular basis. He has also developed a series of displays at the Excel Energy Center, home of the Minnesota Wild, and continues to showcase memorabilia from the Hall at hockey shows and tournaments throughout the country.

Thank you to Ross Bernstein for sharing his passion for our game and for writing and publishing this wonderful new book. Incredibly, Ross has agreed to donate all of his royalties from this book to help in the future development of the Hall. I truly appreciate all of his hard work and his generous gift. He is a true friend to the game of hockey. I also want to thank Duluth sports artist, Tim Cortes, who has graciously allowed us to showcase his newest masterpiece, "Squaw Valley Gold," on the cover of our new book. He is a tremendous talent, and a good friend to the Hall.

In addition, I want to thank the following for all their help and support of the USHHF: The IRRRB, Iron Range Legislators, Cities of Eveleth & Virginia, USA Hockey, The Wild, Pat Forciea, Amy Woog Patnode, Lee Reed, Michelle Putzel, Paulette Pfremmer, Terrence Fogarty and the Board of Directors. I would also like to thank the staff at the Hall for their many hours of extra help through our renovation and also for their dedication and time in gathering information for this publication.

Congratulations to the USHHF Class of 2001: Dave Christian, Paul Johnson and Mike Ramsey, and to the recipient of the Wayne Gretzky Award, Scottie Morrison. All are deserving of recognition for their contributions to the game of hockey, and the Hall is proud to honor their achievements.

Thank you for your continued support.
Jim Findley, President

TABLE OF CONTENTS

3	Cover Art by Tim Cortes	79	Walter Bush, Jr.
4	Introduction	80	Nick Kahler
5	Letter from the President	81	Bob Cleary
7	About the Hall	82	Bill Jennings
10	The Gretzky Award	83	Tommy Williams
11	Gretzky Award '99: Wayne Gretzky	84	Cal Marvin
12	Gretzky Award '00: The Howe Family	85	Bill Stewart
13	Gretzky Award '01: Scotty Morrison	86	Oscar Almquist
14	The History of the Hall	87	Jack McCartan
16	Hockey's Early Roots	88	Billy Christian
23	Mission Statement	89	Bill Wirtz
26	The Hobey Baker Award	90	Bob Blake
27	The Lester Patrick Trophy	91	Dick Rondeau
28	The Inductee's Master List	92	Hal Trumble
29	Taffy Abel	93	Jack Garrity
30	Hobey Baker	94	Ken Yackel
31	Frank Brimsek	95	Jack Kirrane, Jr.
32	George Brown	96	Muzz Murray
33	Walter Brown	97	Richard Desmond
34	John Chase	98	Larry Ross
35	Cully Dahlstrom	99	Roger Christian
36	John Garrison	100	Bob Paradise
37	Doc Gibson	101	Herb Brooks
38	Moose Goheen	102	Willard Ikola
39	Malcolm Gordon	103	Connie Pleban
40	Eddie Jeremiah	104	Robbie Ftorek
41	Mike Karakas	105	Bob Johnson
42	Thomas Lockhart	106	John Matchefts
43	Myles Lane	107	Amo Bessone
44	Sam LoPresti	108	Len Ceglarski
45	John Mariucci	109	James Fullerton
46	George Owen, Jr.	110	Snooks Kelley
47	Ding Palmer	111	Dave Langevin
48	Doc Romnes	112	Charles Schulz
49	Cliff Thompson	113	Joe Cavanagh, Jr.
50	William Thayer Tutt	114	Wally Grant
51	Ralph Winsor	115	Ned Harkness
52	Coddy Winters	116	Henry Boucha
53	Lyle Wright	117	James Claypool
54	Bill Chadwick	118	Ken Morrow
55	Raymond Chaisson	119	Sergio Gambucci
56	Victor Desjardins	120	Reed Larson
57	Doug Everett	121	Craig Patrick
58	Victor Heyliger	122	Charlie Holt
59	Virgil Johnson	123	Bill Nyrop
60	Jack Kelley	124	Tim Sheehy
61	William Moe	125	Mike Curran
62	Fido Purpur	126	Bruce Mather
63	Tony Conroy	127	Joe Mullen
64	Austie Harding, Jr.	128	Lou Nanne
65	Stewart Iglehart	129	Rod Langway
66	Joe Linder	130	Gordie Roberts
67	Frederick Moseley, Jr.	131	Sid Watson
68	Bill Cleary	132	Neal Broten
69	John Mayasich	133	Doug Palazzari
70	Robert Ridder	134	Larry Pleau
71	Earl Bartholome	135	The 1960 U.S. Olympic Team
72	Edward Olson	138	Dave Christian
73	Bill Riley	139	Paul Johnson
74	Peter Bessone	140	Mike Ramsey
75	Donald Clark	141	In Memory of Steven Kirkpatrick
76	Hub Nelson	142	In Memory of Shawn Walsh
77	Bob Dill	143	About the Author, Ross Bernstein
78	Jack Riley, Jr.		

ABOUT THE HALL

The United States Hockey Hall of Fame is America's hockey designated shrine and showcase to all levels of the sport. Since 1973, 110 great Americans with outstanding hockey achievements from all of the competitive levels of the game have been enshrined. Visitors experience the thrilling game action and inspiring achievements of players, coaches, referees, and builders/administrators through authentic, informative and entertaining displays and memorabilia.

Eveleth, Minnesota, "The Capital of American Hockey," has been given that designation and the home of the United States Hockey Hall of Fame because of its rich hockey tradition. No community the size of Eveleth has produced as many quality players or has contributed more to the growth and development of the sport in the US.

Michelle Putzel, Tom Sersha and Paulette Pfremmer

The US Hockey Hall of Fame is a national shrine of historical significance dedicated to honoring the great sport of ice hockey in the United States. From its earliest origins, covering USA Hockey, the National Hockey League and amateur hockey groups, the exhibits will guide you through exciting displays featuring the "Great Wall of Fame" of inductees, the "Olympic Display," "Gallery of Hockey Art," "Theater of Hockey Highlights" and countless historical exhibits of hockey memorabilia.

Honor, Excellence and Commitment. These keywords best describe the recipients of our nation's highest hockey honor. The United States Hockey Hall of Fame is proud to present "The Wall of Fame." The Wall of Fame represents not only the greatest hockey players in the US, but also includes coaches and administrators who helped shape the game of hockey making it one of the fastest growing sports in America.

Enshrinees are nominated by their peers and presented to the nominating committee for election into the Hall of Fame each fall.

For American hockey players, it is the game's highest honor.

Shari Aubol, Ben Squires, Bonnie Vincent and Kathy Trach

THE HEART & SOUL OF THE HALL

Executive Board of Directors
Thomas Micheletti: Chairman of the Board
James Findley: President
Richard Meredith: Executive Vice President
Ray Eck: Treasurer
Brian McCarthy: Secretary
Walter Bush: Board Member/Executive Committee Member
Stanley E. Hubbard II: Board Member/Executive Committee Member
Bob Naegele: Director
Bruce Aho: Director
Brian Burke: NHL

U.S. Hockey Hall of Fame Staff
Tom Sersha: Executive Director
Michelle Putzel: Executive Secretary
Paulette Pfremmer: Gift Shop Manager
Bonnie Vincent, Kathy Trach, Ben Squires
Shari Aubol: Hospitality/Customer Relations
Pat Forciea & Amy Woog Patnode (Messabe Group): Consultants

Board of Governors
Wendell Anderson, Minneapolis, MN
Joseph Begich, Eveleth, MN
John Bernard, Princeton, NJ
George Gund III, San Francisco, CA
John Heneman, Warroad, MN
Farley Karfman, Plymouth, MN
Don Kohlman, Fond Du Lac, WI
Peter Lindberg, Eden Prairie, MN
John Mayasich, Lakeland, MN
Joe Micheletti, Upper Brookville, NY
Lynn Olson, Minneapolis, MN
Jerry Pfremmer, Gilbert, MN
Robert Ridder, Jr., Gross Pointe Farms, MI
Jack Ross, Hibbing, MN
Mike Sertich, Duluth, MN
Frank Sherman, Eveleth, MN
Art Sprague, Columbia, MO
Elmer Walls, Baxter, MN

THE "HALL" OF THE WILD

The National Hockey League's Minnesota Wild and the United States Hockey Hall of Fame have joined together to form a partnership. With it, the Hall has agreed to share many of its exhibits with the organization, to be displayed at the team's new Xcel Energy Center Arena in downtown Saint Paul.

"This partnership strengthens our belief that the new Saint Paul Arena will be the best place to watch hockey in the NHL," said Minnesota Wild President Tod Leiweke. "Fans visiting our Arena will be able to see numerous exhibits featuring the rich history of hockey in the United States."

The Wild Exhibit at the Hall of Fame

Some of the key exhibits that are on display in the main concourse of the new Saint Paul Arena include the 1960 and 1980 U.S. Olympic men's teams and the 1998 Olympic women's team. Other artifacts will include Minnesota hockey memorabilia and displays of prominent U.S. players currently in the Hall of Fame such as: Frank Brimsek, Neal Broten, Moose Goheen, and John Mayasich.

"All of us associated with the Hall of Fame are excited about our new partnership with the Wild," said the Hall's President James Findley. "This relationship not only helps us solidify our long term future in Eveleth but gives us a terrific new opportunity to get exposure in front of millions of professional and amateur hockey fans at the Wild's new arena in Saint Paul."

As part of the agreement, the Wild will also help the Hall of Fame replace exhibits loaned to the new Saint Paul Arena with other traveling exhibits that will be hockey and sports related. The club has also agreed to construct an exhibit within the Arena honoring the city of Eveleth and its history as the home of the Hall of Fame. Over 1.5 million visitors are projected to visit the exhibits in the new Saint Paul Arena each year.

A 1998 Women's Olympic Team exhibit is on display at the "X."

THE GRETZKY AWARD

In 1999 the Hall of Fame proudly unveiled the creation of a new citation called the Wayne Gretzky Award. Given annually to an international citizen who has been deemed to have made a major contribution to the growth and advancement of American hockey, it is one of the Hall's highest honors. Fittingly, the inaugural award was given to its namesake, the "Great One," for his profound effect on the game, particularly in the United States.

Gretzky Award Recipients:

Year	Recipient
1999	Wayne Gretzky
2000	The Gordie Howe Family
2001	Scotty Morrison

THE GRETZKY AWARD 1999: WAYNE GRETZKY

Over his amazing 20-year NHL career, Wayne Gretzky set an amazing 61 records, including 894 goals, 2,857 points and 10 league scoring titles. He grew up in Brantford, Ontario, and by the age of five he was already a prodigy. To honor his idol, No. 9 — Gordie Howe, he even wore No. 99.

After electrifying the junior ranks as a teen-ager, Gretzky turned professional at the age of 17 with the Indianapolis Racers of the World Hockey Association. After eight games Gretzky was traded to the Edmonton Oilers, where he quickly became the talk of hockey rinks around the world. During the 1980's, he simply dominated the game like no one before him. He won the Hart Trophy, as the NHL's most valuable player, nine times, as well as leading the league in scoring seven times.

Following the 1988 season, in one of the biggest trades in sports history, Gretzky was traded to the Los Angeles Kings. Gretzky had an immediate impact not only with his new team, but also with hockey in the U.S. There, he led his Kings to the Stanley Cup Finals in 1993, and became the catalyst of hockey's explosion in popularity throughout the United States.

After a brief stint in St. Louis during the latter part of the 1996 season, Gretzky finished his career in the Big Apple, as a member of the Rangers. He spent three years in New York before retiring in 1999.

Since then, Gretzky has gotten into the administrative side of the game, where he presently serves as a member of the Phoenix Coyotes ownership group.

So amazing was his influence on the game in America, that since he was traded to the Kings back in 1988, the NHL has expanded to 12 new markets. His talent and charisma created a groundswell of interest in the sport that allowed the league to expand to non-traditional hockey markets throughout the country — including in the Sun-Belt.

Equally as important, Gretzky was also very involved with the community and performed countless hours of charity work. As great as he was on the ice, he was as even more outstanding as an ambassador, a hockey humanitarian, a lover of the game and of life. He was truly the "Great One."

Wayne Gretzky

THE GRETZKY AWARD 2000: THE HOWE FAMILY

"Mr. and Mrs. Hockey," Gordie and Colleen Howe, and their sons Mark and Marty, have been chosen to be honored by the U.S. Hockey Hall of Fame for their contributions to the growth of American hockey. Hockey's "First Family" has done so much, both on and off the ice, to advance the game of hockey, that it was only fitting that the they become the first family ever to receive such an honor.

Regarded by many as the greatest player ever, Gordie Howe played 32 brilliant pro seasons that incredibly spanned more than six decades. Gordie was born on March 31, 1928, at Floral, Saskatchewan, and grew up loving the game of hockey. After going on to play one year of minor pro hockey with Omaha, of the USHL, he joined the Detroit Red Wings in 1947, where he became a legend. He had deceptive speed, was physically tough, and was very durable. He was also the ultimate team player, which was why his teammates loved and respected him. By the time he retired in 1980 he had established all-time records for goals (1,071), assists (1,518) and points (2,421). He appeared in an amazing 29 All-Star games, was a seven-time league MVP and finished in the top five in NHL scoring for 20 consecutive seasons.

One of the highlights of his career came in 1974, when he joined up with his two sons, Mark and Marty, as members of the WHA's Houston Aeros, to become the first father-son-son combination in history to play together professionally. The trio went on to make one of the game's greatest lines for seven wonderful seasons — first with Houston, and then with the New England Whalers in 1977, which became the NHL's Hartford Whalers in 1980. Gordie finally hung em up after that season, but, incredibly, made a comeback in 1997 by playing the opening shift for the IHL's Detroit Vipers, thus becoming the first player to appear in a pro game in six decades.

Marty went on to play professionally for 12 years, earning All-Star honors in 1977, and playing for Team Canada in 1975 as well. His younger brother, Mark, also went on to play for 22 years professionally, earning All-Star honors on six occasions, and later leading Team USA to a silver medal in the 1972 Olympics.

The matriarch of the Howe family is "Mrs. Hockey" herself, Colleen. Considered to be the most influential woman in hockey history, she aspired to become the game's first female manager/agent, and also founded the Detroit Jr. Red Wings. In addition, she is the author of the book "My Three Hockey Players," and also co-wrote the book "and...HOWE!", the best-selling hockey hardcover in history. The Howe's have truly earned the title of Hockey's First Family!

Hockey's "First Family" — The Howe's

THE GRETZKY AWARD 2001: SCOTTY MORRISON

One of Hockey's true pioneers, the United States Hockey Hall of Fame is proud to honor Ian "Scotty" Morrison as the third-ever recipient of the coveted Gretzky Award.

Born and educated in Montreal, Quebec, Scotty Morrison played junior hockey with the Montreal Canadiens organization, in the era of Dickie Moore, Jean Beliveau and Boom Boom Geoffrion. After his playing career, Morrison turned to his second passion — officiating, where, over time, he would become one of the game's strongest voices. Morrison first started in the Quebec Amateur Hockey Association, and then moved up to the prestigious Quebec Senior League. In 1952 he was signed by the Western Hockey League and just two years later then NHL Referee-In-Chief, Carl Voss, signed him to his first NHL contract. At just 24 years of age, Morrison became the youngest referee to work in the National Hockey League.

After two seasons in the "Show," Morrison decided to pursue a career in the sales and marketing field, so he moved back to Vancouver, B.C., where he began working with Goodyear Special Products. From there he moved on to Yardley of London, while still continuing to officiate in the WHL. In June of 1965, Scotty was appointed NHL Referee-in-Chief, replacing Carl Voss, who had retired that Spring. By 1981 he named Vice President of Officiating.

In 1986, NHL President John Ziegler appointed Scotty to the position of Vice President of Project Development as well as the President of the Hockey Hall of Fame, in Toronto. In this new position, Scotty was responsible for finding a future site for the Hall and the development of a new Hockey Hall of Fame facility. In October of 1991, Morrison was named as the Chairman and Chief Executive Officer of the Hockey Hall of Fame, and in June of 1993, Morrison's dream finally came to fruition when a beautiful new 50,000 square foot museum and shrine located in historic downtown Toronto was opened for all to see.

Since then Morrison's contributions to the game of hockey have been too numerous to mention. He has been an integral part of the museum and archives world, serving as President of both the Canadian Association of Sports Heritage (C.A.S.H.) and the International Association of Sports Museums and Hall of Fames (IAMSHF).

A recipient of many awards and accolades, Morrison is also an honored enshrinee of the Hockey Hall of Fame as a member of the "Builder" category. Scotty officially retired as Chairman of the Hockey Hall of Fame's Board of Directors on July 31, 1998, but continues to serve as a mentor and friend to the game which he so dearly loves.

Scotty Morrison

THE HISTORY OF THE HALL

Perhaps the most telling sign that Eveleth is indeed the hockey capital of America, is the fact that the US Hockey Hall of Fame is located there. "Why," you might ask, "is a national shrine of this significance dedicated to United States hockey, located in a town of merely 5,000 citizens?" The answer is simple. Eveleth was chosen for its unique long-standing history and incredible contribution to American hockey. And, perhaps most importantly, is the fact that no town of its size has ever produced more elite-level players in the history of the game.

There are several reasons as to why Eveleth is so hockey crazy. In the beginning, the superior Canadian players were imported down to Eveleth to play for the pro teams. In return they were given good paying jobs in the mines. This ultimately served as a wonderful form of entertainment for the miners and their families. Eventually, the game rubbed off on the kids in town who grew up wanting to emulate these new stars, and before they knew it, a whole generation of superstar hockey players was born.

In 1967 an exploratory committee was formed with the idea of creating a United States Hockey Hall of Fame. The idea for the U.S. Hall of Fame was not to compete with the Hockey Hall of Fame in Toronto, rather to celebrate the accomplishments of Americans — in a game that up until recently, was dominated by Canadians.

How the Hall began is an interesting story in itself. In 1967 that committee from the Eveleth Civic Association, known as the "Project H Committee," began an intensive historical search program to determine candidates (other American cities) who they felt were worthy of being host cities to the Hockey Hall of Fame. Their extensive research showed that since the late 1800s, no other town had contributed as much to hockey's development; and no state had contributed more than Minnesota. So, on May 19,1968, they requested the official endorsement from the Amateur Hockey Association of the United States (AHAUS) in Boston, MA. AHAUS, in turn, gave its blessings to the project, and by 1973 the three-story U.S. Hockey Hall of Fame & Museum was completed along Hat Trick Avenue in Eveleth.

The non-profit corporation, United States Hockey

One of the first Zamboni's is on display at the Hall

14

Hall of Fame, Inc. was chartered in the state of Minnesota in 1968 and its first officers and directors included nine members from AHAUS: Robert Ridder, Walter Bush, Don Clark, J. Lawrence Cain, Edward Stanley, Charles Kunkle, Thayer Tutt, Cal Marvin, and Robert Fleming. From the Project H Committee, representing Eveleth, were Larry Doyle, Tony Nemanich, and D. Kelly Campbell. (Campbell, a native of Michigan and a former mining executive with the Ogleby-Norton and Eveleth Taconite Co's, is the person perhaps most responsible for the Hall coming to fruition.)

The Hall of Fame's new Gift Shop

By bringing the past to the present and onto the future, the Hall serves as the focal point for preserving the history and heritage of American Hockey. Today the Hall of Fame is going through a multi-million dollar, three-phase renovation. Working in harmony with USA Hockey, the NHL, and amateur hockey associations throughout Minnesota as well as the United States, the Hall has ensured that hockey fans from around the world will have the type of museum the sport richly deserves well into the 21st century.

"The Hall is really a shrine dedicated to the contributions of those individuals who have helped put the United States on the hockey map with the rest of the world," said Jim Findley, the Hall's President. "Its goal is to celebrate the memories of its enshrinees and their contributions to the game. More and more people are stepping up to help us move forward, and our new renovation project is just fantastic. In judging from the feedback we have already received from our most recent improvements and additions, the Hall will be in excellent shape for many, many years to come."

(Incredibly, nearly 10% of the Hall's inductee's are from Eveleth. Those 12 individuals, which represent more than any other US city, are: Sam LoPresti, Frank Brimsek, Mike Karakas, Oscar Almquist, John Mayasich, John Mariucci, John Matchefts, Willard Ikola, Connie Pleban, Wally Grant, Serge Gambucci and Doug Palazzari.)

The world's biggest hockey stick, downtown Eveleth

HOCKEY'S EARLY ROOTS

To truly understand the modern game of ice hockey today, you have to go back —way back to the very beginning. There we can get to the root of the game's most fundamental origins: ice skating. Now, where and when that beginning actually is, makes for some very interesting debate. We do know, however, that what most likely first started out as a more convenient mode of winter transportation across the slippery ice and snow of frozen lakes and rivers, has evolved over time into what we now know today as ice hockey.

The Ice Game's Evolution
It would seem that most every country through the ages has laid claim to the creation of one form or another of an athletic game. And, the history of advanced games, which involved using a stick to strike an object of some sort, can be traced back for thousands of years. For instance, wall-murals nearly 2,500 years old have been found in Greece which contained carvings portraying two people holding sticks in an athletic-like face-off position, very similar to what we now know as field hockey. Perhaps it was war-like in nature, possibly portraying hand-to-hand combat? Nonetheless, this is one of the ways that sports have evolved.

One such ancient game that may have led to the creation of hockey, was an old British past-time called "camp." Created in the 11th century following the Norman invasions, the game was supposedly started when the local villagers began to imitate how they booted out their intruders, by kicking rocks amongst one another for amusement. Various new games began to develop from this, and not long thereafter different sporting games that involved striking a ball or object with a stick began to emerge. Among them that may have played a part in the genesis of ice hockey over the upcoming millennium would be an amalgam of many different ice and field games including: Shinny, Hurley, Bandy, Baggataway, Ho-Gee, Oochamkunutk, Field Hockey, Lacrosse, Ice Polo, and Kolven.

Ice Bandy

It All Started With Skating
In as early as the 1400s, Northern Europeans and Scandinavians were using not only snowshoes, but also snow skis to get around throughout their harsh winter terrain's. It was not too long

16

after that someone invented the ice skate. It is believed that the first crude form of ice skates were made of small animal bones, which were crudely fastened to one's boots. Later they evolved into wood, which was easier to carve into shape.

There are also many theories as to where the word "skate" came from. Some historians believe that it might be a derivative of the Dutch word "schaat," but there remains a controversy as to who was the first to actually use the new device. Along with the Dutch, all of the Scandinavian countries, as well as the Russians, English, Scottish and Irish, have also laid claim to skating's origins.

In the mid-1500s, the iron skate was finally perfected by Scottish blacksmith's. Soon after, skating became not only a popular form of transit, but also entertainment. In the mid-1600s, the Skating Club of Scotland was established, and other countries followed suit not too long after. When many of these same people migrated across the Atlantic in the early 1800s into North America, they brought their skates with them. Once the sport of ice skating became popular, ice games naturally began to emerge.

Hockey's Early Beginnings
The word hockey seems to be as complex as the game itself. Despite all of the historical research and speculation, nobody really knows for sure who actually invented the game. The most likely scenario is that wherever there were frozen lakes, ponds, rivers, and streams; there were most likely Europeans, Scandinavians, Asians, and North American Indians alike who probably conceived and played some crude form of ice hockey.

One school of thought on how the game got its name came from Great Britain. In as early as 1400, the word hockey was being used in England to describe a field game that was being played by young boys who hauled produce in "hock carts" during harvest festivals. Another theory claims that the word is an English form of the French word "hoquet," which was a shepherd's cane that resembled a modern looking hockey stick. Others claim the word had Native American origins. As far back as the mid-1700s, French explorers who voyaged up the St. Lawrence Seaway, claimed to have seen Iroquois Indians playing a primitive game which entailed using a stick to strike a ball on the ice. When a player hit the ball he would shout out "Ho-Gee," which apparently meant, "it hurts." Yet another school of thought on how hockey got its name came from Canada in the mid-1800s. As the story goes, an English Colonel in the military whose common English fam-

The 1895 Duluth Ice Polo Club

ily name was "Hockey," had his troops playing shinny near Windsor, Ontario, as a form of winter exercise. Supposedly, the game that they were playing became known as "Hockey's game."

Hockey's roots can be traced back to Europe, where in the 1600s the Scottish played a field hockey game called "Shinny," while the Irish played a game known as "Hurley." An additional pastime of this era was a Dutch game played on ice called "Kolven." Played with a ball, and stick that resembled a golf club, one would score a point by hitting the ball between two poles that had been stuck in the ice. Yet another game that was witnessed by French explorers in Canada in the mid-1700s, was an Indian game similar to lacrosse, called "Baggataway."

In the early 1800s, a game called "Bandy" was being played on icy rivers and lakes throughout the marshy Fen region of England. The village of Bury Fen, credited with starting the game, fielded a legendary team that supposedly went more than 100 years without ever losing a match. The game was played on skates with a short curved sticks, called "bandies." They were typically willow tree branches which were cut to the shape of a curved stick. Players used their sticks to strike a "cat," or ball, which was made of wood or cork, and eventually of rubber. Teams consisted of 11 players, and the games began when a referee threw the cat up in the air. The players would quickly fight to grab the cat and dribble it down the enormous 450' x 300' playing surface, and try to shoot it into a large 12-foot-by-7-foot goal. (Incidentally, bandy, which is considered to be the fastest team sport in the world, is currently being played in several places throughout the world including: the former Soviet Union, Scandinavia and also Minnesota. In fact, Minnesota has the only bandy program in the United States, with several leagues and teams playing at rinks in Edina, Roseville, and Bloomington.)

The Evolution of Hockey in North America
As more and more Europeans and Scandinavians migrated to Canada, variations of these games slowly became quite popular on this side of the Atlantic. Hurley, an Irish game, was perhaps the first to be played competitively. One of the ways that the game was brought overseas was from Irish immigrants, who had come to work on the Shubencadie Canal near Dartmouth, Nova Scotia, in the early 1830s. Hurley was a game that was originally played on the grassy fields of Ireland with a brass ball and heavy wooden sticks called "shillelaghs." However, the fields of Eastern Canada's Nova Scotia region were much too rugged to play on, so instead

The 1920 U.S. Olympic Team

they decided to play the game on ice. Soon "Ice Hurley" became the rage at Canada's first college, Windsor's King's College, located near Halifax — which was established in 1788, where students began playing the game competitively on both Long Pond and Chester lakes.

Located on the shores of the Avon River in Nova Scotia, the region was first settled by French Acadian settlers. The Acadians, many of whom were farmers, lived harmoniously with the Mi'kmaq Indians, who were native to the territory. According to the Dictionary of the Language of the Mi'kmaq Indians, which was published in 1888, the Micmac's, as they were known, had invented an ice game of their own which involved using a stick and a ball, called "Oochamkunutk." The Micmac's, who were known for their superior wood-carving abilities, had mastered the art of crafting a one-piece stick. From horubeam trees, and later from second-growth yellow birch trees, these craftsmen could carve powerful, yet durable sticks, or "hockey's" as they became known as, from a single piece of the tree's root. (Later, throughout the early 1920s-30s, the "MicMac" brand evolved into a very high pedigree brand of hockey stick. It become the most popular manufactured stick of its kind in hockey, and by 1925 it was being advertised and sold around the world for a whopping .50¢ to .75¢ apiece.)

The Micmac's, who referred to ice hurley as "Alchamadijik," would gradually join with both the Acadians as well as the British soldiers in playing pick up games with one another. Slowly their games began to rub off on each other, and melded together. With an unlimited number of players out on the ice, some of them competed in wooden skates, while others simply wore moccasins. The games got rough, and for protection, the Micmac's used moose skin for padding on their shins and arms. Their new Canadian style of hurley featured sticks which they called "hurley's" to hit a square wooden block, through a goal. As time went by, ice hurley was referred to by many names, including: Hurley, Ricket, Cricket, and Wicket.

Long considered to be hockey's predecessor, "Shinny" was yet another informal ice game of the mid-1800s to evolve from the United Kingdom to North America. The game's rules were directly related to English field hockey, hurley, and lacrosse. The object of the game is very similar to today's hockey, in which opposing players tried to shoot a block of wood or a rubber ball into a goal, commonly made from two rocks or even tin cans, which served as markers. With no

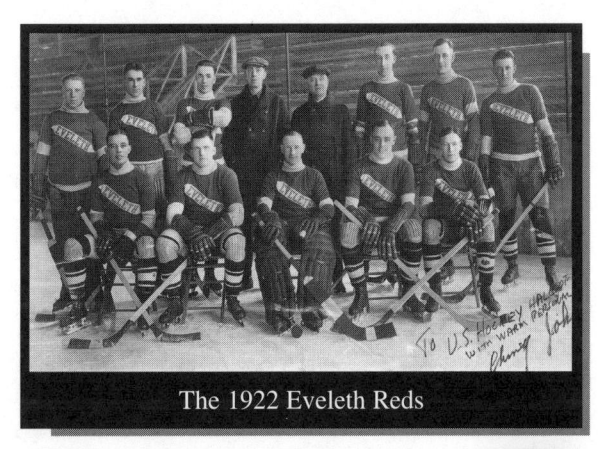

The 1922 Eveleth Reds

The 1924 Eveleth High School Squad

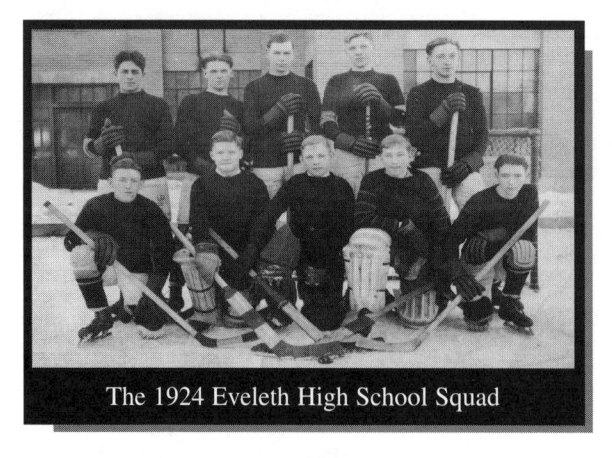

set time limits, games were played on huge rinks that were formed in rivers, lakes, ponds, and creeks. Spectators could often-times be seen cheering for their teams by running up and down the river banks. There were no side boards of any type, so much of the games were spent chasing after the ball. One of the game's most prominent rules was taken directly from field hockey, in which during a face-off, or "bully" as it was called, players had to "shinny on their own side," which meant they had to take the draw right-handed.

Considered by some to be the greatest winter sport in North America, Shinny, or shinty, became quite popular throughout Canada and parts of the Northern United States in the mid to late 1800s. Many kids played in their boots if they didn't own a pair of ice skates of their own. Kids used to scour the forests to find a good "shinny stick" to play with. They would look for a solid branch from an old maple, oak, or ash tree, which might have a slight crook or growth at the end of it which would form a blade. (A good shinny stick was so durable that players would occasionally pass their sticks down generationally to their own kids.) And, getting whacked on the shins, or anywhere else for that matter, was just part of the game. The referees typically ignored slashing, roughing, high sticking, and cross checking. Rather he would holler out the cry, "Shinny on your own side!" which was also a warning to settle down. Sometimes if a player didn't cool off, the ref would simply whack him across the shins. Most kids came home with torn trousers, and most likely, bruised shins.

While there is much debate as to whether or not the first ever hockey games played in Canada, were in fact shinny games, yet one more ice game evolved in the late 1800s after shinny and before ice hockey, called "Ice Polo." Besides shinny, it is believed that the forerunner to ice hockey in the US was ice polo, an American conception that was probably adopted from the popular fad-sport

Women's Hockey in 1925

of roller polo — which was played in indoor roller rinks. Played much like football on ice, only with a hard rubber ball, ice polo teams featured a goaltender, a halfback, a center and two rushers. Ice polo was being played on outdoor ice by the late 1870's in parts of Minnesota, New England, and Michigan. Beginning in 1883, there was even a four team ice polo league playing in St. Paul which sponsored annual tournaments at the infamous St. Paul Winter Carnival. But, by the early 1900's ice hockey had replaced ice polo in the US.

Eveleth's Legendary Hippodrome

The Modern Game

As the present-day game of ice hockey started to take shape from bits and pieces of its many unique predecessors, it can safely be said that Canada is the modern game's originator. It is believed that a refined game of shinny, which included many of modern hockey's rules and characteristics, was first played in 1855 on a harbor just outside Halifax, Nova Scotia, by members of an Imperial Army unit known as "Her Majesty's Royal Canadian Rifles."

Much of the credit for the rules of the modern game have been credited to a gentleman named, J.G.H. Creighton, of Halifax, who, in the 1850s, combined the rules of British field hockey, shinny, and ice lacrosse to form the basis of ice hockey. Several rule changes were starting to be introduced to the game, including: reducing the number of players on the ice from eleven to seven players, incorporating a standard 3" x 1" puck — instead of a ball — and also creating short side boards around the ice surfaces. In addition, ice rinks were popping up all around the countrysides. (The term rink, which referred to the designated area of play, and also meant race-course, was originally used in the game of curling in 18th-century Scotland.)

Others debate that the first real hockey game, with more defined rules and with a limited number of players, was actually played

The 1945 State High School Champs from Eveleth

in 1875 at the indoor Victoria Skating Rink, by McGill University students in Montreal. (Incidentally, for this game, J.G.A. Creighton ordered and shipped two dozen MicMac hockey sticks to his friends in Halifax for their big game against McGill in Montreal.) Here, hockey grew and prospered. The early playing style seemed to accentuate a more rugged playing style, versus a finesse game. But, as time went by and more and more people began playing, stickhandling, passing and skating became much more refined. During this period at the University, there is also speculation that several football coaches incorporated many of the rules of rugby into the game — which may explain for the game's rough style of play.

By the mid-1880s, hockey leagues were being played between both coasts throughout Canada. Nearly every small town had teams which played against one another, and kids began to learn how to skate as soon as they could learn how to walk. The sport of ice hockey became a recognized sport, and in 1883, also an official event at the Montreal Winter Carnival. The carnival committee even issued a challenge for the "world championship" of ice hockey, as teams from Quebec, Ottawa, Toronto, and Montreal answered the call to play in what is believed to be the first ice hockey tournament in the world. An interesting refinement came to the game by way of the Winter Carnival a few years later in 1886. That was when one of the teams showed up for the tournament short a pair of players. The other team felt compelled to help out their opponents, and thereby agreed to drop two of their skaters to make it even. The teams found that with four less men on the ice, they could really open up the play and spread things out. And with that, the nine-man game finally gave way to the seven-man game.

Shortly thereafter, in 1886, representatives from several Canadian teams gathered together to finally establish a formal set of rules for consistent play against one-another. What they came up with would become known as the "Montreal Rules." A governing body was formed, and they called themselves the Canadian Amateur Hockey League (the predecessor to today's Canadian Amateur Hockey Association). They called for seven-man hockey, which featured a goaltender, two half-backs (who played close to the goal like a modern defenseman), a rover, and three forwards. Players became quite proficient in stickhandling, because back then there was no forward passing allowed. Any forward pass was immediately ruled off-sides. Games consisted of two half-hour periods, with a ten minute breather in-between to shovel the ice.

The 1972 U.S. Olympic Team

Hockey America

America's hockey roots are not quite as complicated as those of Canada's, but nonetheless, there is some debate as to where and when the game migrated southward below the 49th parallel. The American concoction known as ice polo, muddied up the waters with regards to determining the exact origins of the game in the US. While some say the game started officially on the East Coast, an argument can be made that the game was also being played at the same time right here in Minnesota. One of those theories, however, takes us back to the Summer of 1894, to Niagara Falls, New York.

There, a group of American tennis players from Yale University were competing in a tournament with some players from Canada. In between the competition, some of the players began socializing, and talking about winter ice games. Upon learning that the Americans were still playing ice polo, the Canadians, who were playing ice hockey, invited their new American friends up north of the border that upcoming winter to play a friendly exhibition of both sports. They agreed, and played a series of two-period, double-headers of each game throughout several major Canadian cities in front of capacity crowds. Upon the conclusion of the contests, the Canadians had swept the hockey games, while the Yanks won two and tied two of the ice polo games. When it was all said and done, the Americans agreed that ice hockey was a much better game to play. Instantly enamored with their new-found game, the American boys bought up all of the sticks and skates that they could carry and returned home. Upon their arrival, they began to play hockey full-time, which included switching over to using flat-bottom skates, a puck — instead of a ball, and a longer hockey-styled stick instead of the field hockey kind. Within a couple of years, most of the universities and club teams up and down the East Coast had switched from ice polo to the faster and more exciting sport of ice hockey.

At about the same time that the East-Coasters were getting indoctrinated to the game of ice hockey, the game was also being spread southward into the US from other points of Canada as well. Which is why at about the same time during the late 1890s, the game was also being played in both Minneapolis, St. Paul, and also in parts of Northern Minnesota, including: Eveleth. In addition, the University of Minnesota

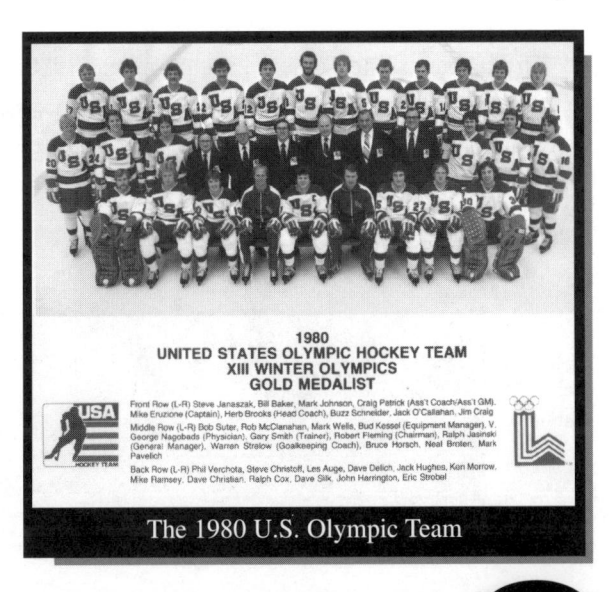

The 1980 U.S. Olympic Team

The Hall of Fame's Mariucci Statue

began playing ice hockey in 1895 against several teams from Canada, including Winnipeg.

America's first big-time league, the Amateur Hockey League, began play in New York City in 1896, and just months later the Baltimore Hockey League got started. In 1899 the Intercollegiate Hockey League was formed with teams from Yale, Columbia, Brown, Harvard, and Princeton. In addition, high school and prep school hockey was being played by the early 1900's in Minnesota, New York City, New England, and in Michigan's Upper Peninsula. The sport continued to grow in America to cities throughout the East Coast and Midwest. In 1903, the International Pro Hockey League became the USA's first professional circuit. Michigan's Upper Peninsula mining town team of Houghton, called the Portage Lakers, became the first professional team in the United States. Now legendary, this club often-times whipped their Canadian counterparts, and helped to put American hockey on the map.

Then, a forerunner of the National Hockey Association, which began play in 1909, the present-day (six-man style) National Hockey League was created in 1917. That same year the Seattle Metropolitans, members of Canada's Pacific Coast League, became the first US team to win the Stanley Cup in its 24-year-old history, greatly embarrassing the Canadian clubs who didn't give the American teams much respect. Oh how the game has changed!

Hockey has truly come a long way in America, and as we head into the new millennium, the game only continues to get better and better.

The United States Hockey Hall of Fame, Eveleth, Minnesota

MISSION STATEMENT

The United States Hockey Hall of Fame, the national shrine of American hockey, is dedicated to honoring the sport of ice hockey in the United States by preserving those precious memories and legends of the game, on all levels, with programs that capture the true spirit and excitement of the sport it represents.

EXPERIENCE HISTORY!

The United States Hockey Hall of Fame is located in Eveleth, Minn., only three hours north of the Twin Cities, in the heart of the historic Iron Range. A perfect vacation stop for the whole family, Eveleth, is a gateway to the great Northern Minnesota wilderness areas and also to majestic Lake Superior.

United States Hockey Hall of Fame
801 Hat Trick Avenue
P.O. Box 657
Eveleth, Minnesota 55734
1-800-HHF-PUCK

Hours of Operation: 9-5 Monday-Saturday • 10-3 Sundays

Admission:
$6.00 for Adults
$5.00 for Senior Citizens
$5.00 for Youth 13 to 17
$4.00 for Children 6 to 12
(Children five and under are free)

THE HOBEY BAKER AWARD

Each April the nation's best collegiate hockey player receives the Hobey Baker Award, college hockey's equivalent to the Heisman Trophy. The recipient is the player who best exemplifies the qualities that Hobey Baker himself demonstrated as an athlete at Princeton University in the early 1900s. Baker was considered to be the ultimate sportsman who despised foul play — picking up only two penalties in his entire college hockey career. With his speed and superior stick handling, Baker opened up the game of hockey and set new standards for the way the game was played. A true gentleman, his habit of insisting upon visiting each opponent's locker room after every game to shake their hands became a model for today's players. A hero, Baker gave his life as an American pilot in W.W.I.

In 1981 Bloomington's Decathlon Club founded the Hobey Baker Memorial Award and each year presents the coveted honor to the nation's top skater. The nation's top hockey coaches, players, media and fans from around the country, as well as the finalists themselves, fly in to attend the gala event. The club also commissioned a Twin Cities sculptor, Bill Mack, to create its beautiful signature trophy, simply known as the "Hobey." The balloting for the award is voted on by the nearly 50 NCAA D-I coaches who are asked to pick the top three players in their league as well as the top three in the nation.

(In addition, in 1998 the USA Hockey Foundation created the annual *Patty Kazmaier Memorial Award*, which recognizes the accomplishments of the outstanding player in women's collegeiate hockey. Past recipients include: Brandy Fisher, New Hampshire (1998), A.J. Mleczko, Harvard (1999), Ali Brewer, Brown (2000) and Jennifer Botterill, Harvard (2001).

Past Hobey Baker Memorial Award Recipients:

Year	Recipient	School
2001	Ryan Miller	Michigan State
2000	Mike Mottau	Boston College
1999	Jason Krog	New Hampshire
1998	Chris Drury	Boston University
1997	Brendan Morrison	University of Michigan
1996	Brian Bonin	University of Minnesota
1995	Brian Holzinger	Bowling Green State University
1994	Chris Marinucci	University of Minnesota-Duluth
1993	Paul Kariya	University of Maine
1992	Scott Pellerin	University of Maine
1991	David Emma	Boston College
1990	Kip Miller	Michigan State University
1989	Lane MacDonald	Harvard University
1988	Robb Stauber	University of Minnesota
1987	Tony Hrkac	University of North Dakota
1986	Scott Fusco	Harvard University
1985	Bill Watson	University of Minnesota-Duluth
1984	Tom Kurvers	University of Minnesota-Duluth
1983	Mark Fusco	Harvard University
1982	George McPhee	Bowling Green State University
1981	Neal Broten	University of Minnesota

THE LESTER PATRICK TROPHY

The Lester Patrick Trophy is an award given annually for outstanding service to hockey in the United States. Eligible recipients are players, officials, coaches, executives, and referees. The winner is selected by an award committee consisting of the President of the NHL, an NHL Governor, a representative of the New York Rangers, a member of the Hockey Hall of Fame Builder's section, a member of the Hockey Hall of Fame Player's section, a member of the U. S. Hockey Hall of Fame, a member of the NHL Broadcasters' Association, and a member of the Professional Hockey Writers' Association. Except the NHL President, each member is rotated annually.

The Patrick Trophy was presented by the New York Rangers in 1966 to honor the late Lester Patrick — the longtime famed general manager and coach of the team.

Year	*Recipients*
2001	Gary Bettman, Scotty Bowman, David Poile
2000	Mario Lemieux, Craig Patrick, Lou Vairo
1999	Harry Sinden, U.S. Women's Olympic Team
1998	Peter Karmanos, Neal Broten, John Mayasich, Max McNab
1997	Seymour H. Knox III, Bill Cleary, Pat LaFontaine
1996	George Gund, Ken Morrow, Milt Schmidt
1995	Joe Mullen, Brian Mullen, Bob Fleming
1994	Wayne Gretzky, Robert Ridder
1993	*Frank Boucher, *Mervyn (Red) Dutton, Bruce McNall, Gil Stein
1992	Al Arbour, Art Berglund, Lou Lamoriello
1991	Rod Gilbert, Mike Ilitch
1990	Len Ceglarski
1989	Dan Kelly, Lou Nanne, *Lynn Patrick, Bud Poile
1988	Keith Allen, Fred Cusick, Bob Johnson
1987	*Hobey Baker, Frank Mathers
1986	John MacInnes, Jack Riley
1985	Jack Butterfield, Arthur M. Wirtz
1984	John A. Ziegler Jr., *Arthur Howie Ross
1983	Bill Torrey
1982	Emile P. Francis
1981	Charles M. Schulz
1980	Bobby Clarke, Edward M. Snider, Frederick A. Shero, The U.S. Olympic Team
1979	Bobby Orr
1978	Phil Esposito, Tom Fitzgerald, William T. Tutt, William W. Wirtz
1977	John P. Bucyk, Murray A. Armstrong, John Mariucci
1976	Stanley Mikita, George A. Leader, Bruce A. Norris
1975	Donald M. Clark, William L. Chadwick, Thomas N. Ivan
1974	Alex Delvecchio, Murray Murdoch, *Weston W. Adams Sr., *Charles L. Crovat
1973	Walter L. Bush Jr.
1972	Clarence S. Campbell, John A. Kelly, Ralph Cooney Weiland, *James D. Norris
1971	William M. Jennings, *John B. Sollenberger, *Terrance G. Sawchuk
1970	Edward W. Shore, *James C.V. Hendy
1969	Robert M. Hull, *Edward J. Jeremiah
1968	Thomas F. Lockhart, *Walter A. Brown, *Gen. John R. Kilpatrick
1967	Gordon Howe, *Charles F. Adams, *James Norris Sr.
1966	J.J. (Jack) Adams

awarded posthumously

THE HALL OF FAME'S ENSHRINEES

1973
Taffy Abel
Hobey Baker
Frank Brimsek
George Brown
Walter Brown
John Chase
Cully Dahlstrom
John Garrison
Doc Gibson
Moose Goheen
Malcolm Gordon
Eddie Jeremiah
Mike Karakas
Tom Lockhart
Myles Lane
Sam LoPresti
John Mariucci
George Owen
Ding Palmer
Doc Romnes
Cliff Thompson
Thayer Tutt
Ralph Winsor
Coddy Winters
Lyle Wright

1974
Bill Chadwick
Ray Chiasson
Vic Desjardins
Doug Everett
Vic Heylinger
Virgil Johnson
Snooks Kelley
Bill Moe
Fido Purpur

1975
Tony Conroy
Austie Harding
Stewart Iglehart
Joe Linder
Fred Moseley

1976
Bill Cleary
John Mayasich
Bob Ridder

1977
Earl Bartholome
Eddie Olson
Bill Riley

1978
Peter Bessone
Don Clark
Hub Nelson

1979
Bob Dill
Jack Riley

1980
Walter Bush
Nick Kahler

1981
Bob Cleary
Bill Jennings
Tommy Williams

1982
Cal Marvin
Bill Stewart

1983
Oscar Almquist
Jack McCartan

1984
William Christian
William Wirtz

1985
Bob Blake
Dick Rondeau
Hal Trumble

1986
Jack Garrity
Ken Yackel

1987
Jack Kirrane
Hugh "Muzz" Murray, Sr.

1988
Richard Desmond
Lawrence Ross

1989
Roger Christian
Robert Paradise

1990
Herb Brooks
Willard Ikola
Connie Pleban

1991
Robbie Ftorek
Robert Johnson
John Matchefts

1992
Amo Bessone
Len Ceglarski
James Fullerton

1993
John Kelley
David Langevin
Charles Schulz

1994
Joe Cavanagh
Wally Grant
Ned Harkness

1995
Henry Boucha
James Claypool
Ken Morrow

1996
Sergio Gambucci
Reed Larson
Craig Patrick

1997
Charles Holt, Jr
William Nyrop
Timothy Sheehy

1998
Mike Curran
Joe Mullen
Bruce Mather
Lou Nanne

1999
Rod Langway
Gordy Roberts
Sid Watson

2000
Neal Broten
Doug Palazzari
Larry Pleau
1960 U.S. Olympic Team

2001
Dave Christian
Paul Johnson
Mike Ramsey

THE INAUGURAL CLASS OF 1973

Clarence J. "Taffy" Abel

New York Rangers & Chicago Blackhawks (1926-1934)
Defenseman
Born: May 28, 1900, Sault Ste. Marie, Mich.

Taffy Abel knew his finest moments while wearing the uniform of the New York Rangers and Chicago Blackhawks in an era when the National Hockey League was scrambling from an offbeat collection of muscular mavericks to a solid organization. Abel's fabulous climb from Sault Ste. Marie amateur ranks to the NHL stamped him as a legend in hockey. He left an indelible imprint in pro and amateur circles as a player, coach and manager. Taffy Abel was a name beloved by hockey followers across the continent in the era of the 60-minute men. He played his first game in Sault Ste. Marie in 1918, and carried the American flag as he took the Olympic oath for hockey players in Chamonix, France, in 1924. After a stint with the Minneapolis Millers during the 1925-26 season, he joined the original New York Rangers when the club made its NHL debut (1926-27). Here Taffy played alongside rugged Ivan "Ching" Johnson on the blue line. The first-year Ranger team won its division title and the next year claimed the Stanley Cup.

The 1928 Stanley Cup series against the Montreal Maroons was a memorable one in the life of Taffy Abel, for it was during a game in that series that he rose to national acclaim. The goalie for the Rangers was hit in the head with a shot and was removed from the ice on a stretcher. After an attempt by the Rangers to sign a goalie from the stands was nullified, Ranger Manager Lester Patrick donned the pads and stood between the pipes. Abel and Johnson allowed only three shots to be fired at Patrick, playing his first game ever in the nets. Abel also was a member of the 1933-34 Stanley Cup-winning Chicago Blackhawks.

For many years Abel was the only American-born player in the NHL and at one point, with the Hawks, set an NHL record when he played 100 minutes in a series against Les Canadians without a substitution.

Taffy Abel

Hobart A. H. "Hobey" Baker

Princeton University (1911-1914)

Forward

Born: January 15, 1892, Wissahickon, Penn.

Hobey Baker

"Like his contemporaries Jim Thorpe, Ty Cobb, and Jack Johnson, Hobey Baker was a fabulous athlete. Like them, he had a great physique, fantastic reflexes, instant coordination of hand and eye, iron discipline and blazing courage. But to these rare abilities he added another dimension all his own...to the public during his career at Princeton and St. Nick's he was the college athlete supreme: the gentlemen sportsman, the amateur in the pure sense playing the game "Pour le sport, who never fowled, despised publicity, and refused professional offers." So wrote John Davis in his biography, "The Legend of Hobey Baker." Baker learned early in life the arts of both stickhandling and skating. He was a master at both.

Davies describes his play best when he relates: "It was the age of seven man hockey, no forward passing and no substitutions; he played the position of rover, the offensive superstar permitted to roam all over the ice. The typical play was for him to take a rebound at his own end, circle the goal to pick up speed, and then tear down the length of the ice, by the rules unable to forward pass; because of the no-substitution rule and his phenomenal endurance, this went on all night. Because of the further accident that Princeton at the time had no rink of its own, he always played in cities before big crowds; whenever he got the puck and took off, the crowd would jump to its feet and shout, "Here he comes!". Prior to entering Princeton in 1910 Baker attended the St. Paul's School, Concord, New Hampshire where Malcom K. Gordon, another United States Hockey Hall of Fame enshrinee was the coach.

At Princeton he was not only a legend in hockey, but in football as well. He captained the hockey team for two years and the football team for one. In his senior year he even drop-kicked a 43-yard field goal to tie Yale. After leaving Princeton Baker continued in hockey with the St. Nicholas Club until his entry into the famed United States flying unit, the Lafayette Esquadrille, in World War I. He was killed in a tragic air accident shortly after the end of the war. He was later honored by having an award, the Hobey Baker Memorial Award, given annually to the nation's top collegiate player — a gesture fitting of the type of first-class person both on and off the ice that he was.

Frank C. "Mr. Zero" Brimsek

Boston Bruins (1938-1945)
Chicago Blackhawks (1946-1950)

Goaltender

Born: Sept. 26, 1915, Eveleth, Minn.

Frank Brimsek's star flashed on the National Hockey League scene with an initial brilliance few rookies have ever matched. Coming up from Providence in the fall of 1938, he replaced the great Cecil "Tiny" Thompson in the Boston Bruins net and proceeded to blank the opposition in six of his first eight games. This performance immediately gained Brimsek the dubious nickname of "Mr. Zero."

Frank Brimsek

He went on that season to win the Calder Trophy as the outstanding rookie and the Vezina Trophy as the league's leading goalie. The Bruins proceeded to capture the Stanley Cup that season as well as in 1941. Brimsek was one of the many players produced by Coach Cliff Thompson, also a United States Hockey Hall of Fame enshrinee, at Eveleth High School. After graduating from Eveleth High School, Brimsek played for what is now St. Cloud State University before launching his post college career with the amateur Pittsburgh Yellow Jackets in 1935-36. He played one full season in Providence of the then International American League, before the call came to Boston.

Brimsek captured another Vezina Trophy in 1942 and then served two years in the Coast Guard during World War II. While in the service he played for the Coast Guard Cutters team which played in the Eastern Amateur Hockey League and was made up of some outstanding American pros. Returning from World War II Brimsek played until 1950, his last season with Chicago, before retiring.

In addition to his two Vezina trophies, he was a first team All Star on two occasions and a six-time second team All Star as well. In addition, he also played in two All Star games. Over 10 seasons of regular and playoff action, Brimsek's goals against average was 2.74 with 42 shutouts. He was also selected to the Hockey Hall of Fame in Toronto in 1966, an honor reserved for just a handful of Americans.

George V. Brown

Boston Athletic Club
Boston Arena
Boston Gardens
(1910-1937)

Administrator

Born: October 21, 1880, Boston, Mass.

In 1910 the Boston Arena was built and with it the Boston Athletic Association (BAA) hockey team. George Brown was the driving force behind this team which played top amateur clubs in the Eastern United States as well as leading Canadian and college teams. When the Arena burned down in 1918, Brown formed the corporation which constructed the new Arena. He then managed both the new building as well as continuing the BAA team. This club formed the basis of the 1924 United States Olympic Team with seven of the ten players BAA members. The United States finished second, losing only to Canada 6-1 in the finals.

Brown was not initially involved in professional hockey, but once Boston secured a National Hockey League franchise, the first United States city to do so, it was not long before he was part of the professional scene. When the Bruins moved into the new Boston Gardens in 1928 he helped organize the Canadian-American League, a forerunner to the present American Hockey League, and entered the Boston Tigers in the league. Brown became general manager of both the Arena and Boston Gardens in 1934. Continuing his roll as an American hockey pioneer, he continually boosted the game at all levels.

Tom Hines the founder of the Massachusetts State High School Hockey Tournament recalls Brown's great foresight regarding high school hockey. "I told George V. Brown....when he was in charge of the Boston Arena we didn't make very much money in that first go. He said not to worry about it. He felt high school hockey would someday fill Boston Arena. I guess he was right. It's now filling Boston Gardens."

Brown continued in his positions with the Arena and Gardens until his death in 1937. He was selected as a member of the Hockey Hall of Fame in Toronto in 1961.

Walter A. Brown

Boston Gardens
Boston Bruins
International Ice Hockey Federation
(1933-1964)

Administrator

Born: February 10, 1905, Boston, Mass.

Following in the footsteps of his father George Brown, also an enshrinee of the United States Hockey Hall of Fame, Walter Brown made great and significant contributions to American hockey, particularly in the area of the international game. Brown coached the Boston Olympics senior team between 1930 and 1940 and won five United States national amateur championships. The pinnacle was reached in 1933 when this team captured the World Championships at Prague as representatives of the United States. Brown arranged a vigorous exhibition schedule for this team both before and after the five-game World Championship series. All told, including the World Championships, the team won 44, lost 3, and tied 3. Playing on this team were United States Hockey Hall of Fame enshrinees John Chase, John Garrison and Ding Palmer.

Brown succeeded his father as general manager of Boston Gardens in 1937 and continued a policy of strong support for hockey in the schools and colleges. As the years passed his involvement with hockey became deeper, and at the time of his death he was president of the Boston Gardens, member of the Hockey Hall of Fame (Toronto) Governing Committee, co-owner and president of the Boston Bruins, and past president of the International Ice Hockey Federation.

In 1960, as chairman of the United States Olympic Ice Hockey Committee he played a significant role in the selection of the gold medal winning United States team.

In resolution at its 1965 convention in Madison, Wis., the Amateur Hockey Association of the United States said it all: "...pays tribute to his outstanding devotion to the Amateur Hockey Association of the United States, and recognizes the leadership that Mr. Brown, over the great many years, gave to the development of amateur hockey in the United States and throughout the world."

Walter Brown

John P. Chase

Harvard University (1924-1928)

Forward

Born: June 12, 1906, Milton, Mass.

John Chase began his formal hockey career at Milton Academy playing on the 1922-23 team. Transferring to Exeter Academy the following year he played there one year before matriculating at Harvard in the fall of 1924. At Harvard, Chase's strength and skill as a hockey player soared.

He played as a regular at center ice as a freshman and as a first line center on the varsity for three years. He was selected as team captain his senior year. Chase also excelled at baseball at Harvard and as an amateur player in later years.

Following graduation from Harvard, Chase was sought after by professional teams, but he chose instead to pursue a business career. He did, however, continue his hockey career with such teams as the Boston Athletic Association, Boston University Club, and Brac Burn Hockey Club. All were strong contenders because of Chase's presence in the lineup.

In 1932 he captained the United States Olympic Team which captured the silver medal at Lake Placid, NY, losing the final game to Canada 2-1 in a heartbreaker. When his playing days were over Chase coached the Harvard varsity for eight years, from 1942 through 1950. Not only was John Chase a graceful, heady player and playmaker, he was also a very talented coach.

Carl S. "Cully" Dahlstrom

Chicago Blackhawks (1937-1945)

Forward

Born: July 3, 1913, Minneapolis, Minn.

Cully Dahlstrom played high school hockey at Minneapolis South and then went on to play for the Minneapolis Millers in the American Hockey Association. The AHA was a strong minor professional league of that time and sent many promising players into the National Hockey League.

It was there that he caught the eye of Major Fred McLaughlin of the Chicago Blackhawks, who was always on the lookout for promising American talent. Dahlstrom didn't let McLaughlin down as he won the Calder Trophy as the National Hockey League's rookie of the year in 1938. In the semi-final playoffs against the New York Americans he scored the winning goal in 1-0 overtime victory in the second game. In the finals against Toronto he scored the key first goal in the 4-1 victory which brought the Stanley Cup to the Windy City.

In the 1940-41 Stanley Cup playoffs Dahlstrom once again had a strong series against the Montreal Canadiens. He scored once in a 4-3 loss and then won the series for the Hawks with two goals in the final 3-2 victory. Chicago was subsequently eliminated by Detroit. Dahlstrom ultimately decided to retire after the 1945 season.

Appearing in 368 regular and playoff games he scored 94 goals and 126 assists. Dahlstrom's most outstanding single season was 1943-44 when he scored 20 goals and 22 assists in the then 50 game schedule.

John B. Garrison

Harvard University (1928-32)
U.S. Olympic Teams (1932 & 1936)

Forward - Defenseman

U.S. Olympic Team (1948)

Coach

Born: Feb. 13, 1909, West Newton, Mass.

John Garrison

John Garrison grew up playing hockey in his native West Newton. There, he attended the local Country Day School, and as a school boy there had the unparalleled record of playing six years on the varsity!

He then went on to Harvard, where he was a regular on the freshman team and then a varsity regular for three seasons at center ice.
Garrison was adept at any forward position as well as on defense. Professional hockey also sought out Garrison, as it did his teammate John Chase before him, but like Chase, Garrison preferred to stake out a career in the business world.

Amateur and international hockey, however, continued to have a demand on his hockey talents. During the 1930's he starred on several amateur teams which went on to win United States national titles. During these years he gained the reputation as one of the finest amateur players in the nation.

Garrison also played defense for the 1932 United States Olympic Team which captured a silver medal at Lake Placid. In addition, in 1933, at Prague, Czechoslovakia, he scored an unassisted overtime goal against Canada to give the United States a 2-1 victory, and its first World Championship. He then went on to captain the 1936 Olympic Team as well, which won a bronze medal at Garmish. He rounded out his brilliant international hockey career by serving as the coach of the 1948 United States Olympic Team.

He went on to use his Harvard education wisely and later became a very successful businessman as well. He was a good friend to the sport of hockey, and should be regarded as one of the game's early innovators and pioneers of both playing and coaching techniques.

John L. "Doc" Gibson

International Hockey League
(1903-1907)

Administrator

Born: September 10, 1880, Ontario, Canada.

Gibson, a graduate of the Detroit Medical School, was a fine player in Canada and was prevailed upon by the late Merv Youngs, then a cub reporter and later editor of the Houghton Mining Gazette, to join the Portage Lake (Houghton-Hancock) organization. Gibson was a native of Berlin, Ontario, now Kitchener. The new hockey team, fashioned by the late James R. Dee, was built around Gibson as captain. It was called the Portage Lakers. Their fame reached into Canada and soon they had gained recognition for the roughest, toughest hockey in the world.

In 1903 a four-team league flourished in the Upper Peninsula (Houghton, Hancock, Laurium, and American Sault). Then, in 1903-04, Canadian players began drifting into the Copper Country, including such greats as Riley Hern, Hod and Bruce Stuart and Cyclone Taylor. Gibson was instrumental in forming these players into the first professional league in the world, the International Hockey League, of which Portage Lake was a member. Gibson was the team's leading scorer, although there is no record of his exact number of goals. The 1903-04 Portage Lake team was perhaps one of the greatest hockey teams of all times. In 26 games it scored 273 goals and allowed only 48. Only twice were they defeated — by the American Soo, 7-6, in the regular season, and by Pittsburgh, 5-2, in U.S. playoffs. Then the Lakers beat Pittsburgh, 5-1 and 7-0, for the American Championship.

Later, at Houghton where over 5,000 fans packed the Old Amphidrome, Portage Lake defeated the Montreal Wanderers, 8-4 and 9-2, to lay claim to the world championship. Other teams which bowed to the Portage Lakers were St. Paul, Detroit, Grand Rapids, Cleveland, St. Louis and the Canadian Soo.

In the spring of 1905 Portage Lake sent word to the Stanley Cup committee Board of Governors challenging the Ottawa Silver Seven to a championship series, and in 1906 they did the same to Montreal. Both refused. It was then that the Canadian clubs signed away the great Portage Lake Players and Gibson returned to Canada to enter the medical profession.

Francis F. "Moose" Goheen

St. Paul Athletic Club (1915-1917)
St. Paul Saints (1920-1932)

Defenseman

Born: Feb. 9, 1894, White Bear Lake, Minn.

Moose Goheen learned his hockey on the outdoor rinks of White Bear Lake and nearby St. Paul. He was not only a great hockey but also an outstanding football and baseball performer as well. In the fall of 1915 Goheen joined the St. Paul Athletic Club, one of the strongest American amateur teams of its time.

Moose Goheen

Goheen, along with such other greats as Tony Conroy, Cy Weidenborner and Ed Fitzgerald, helped capture the McNaughton Trophy in 1916-17. This trophy, now in the hands of the Western Collegiate Hockey Association, was then symbolic of American amateur hockey supremacy. St. Paul won the cup again the following year as well as the Art Ross Cup from Lachine, Quebec in Montreal.

Goheen then joined the U.S. Army for World War I service. Returning in 1920 Moose Goheen led the St. Paul team to another McNaughton Trophy. He joined the first United States Olympic Hockey team in the same year. Playing at Antwerp, Belgium, the United States skaters won three by wide margins and lost only to Canada for a second place silver medal finish. These games were the only Olympic competition in which seven-man hockey was played. Goheen was unable to play for the 1924 team because of business commitments. He continued with the St. Paul team through 1926 when it turned professional and then on through 1932.

Goheen was drafted by the Boston Bruins, and also offered a contract by the Toronto Maple Leafs, but preferred to remain in Minnesota where he was an executive with the Northern States Power Company. Among his many contributions to the game, he is credited with originating the wearing of helmets to protect sustained injuries. On the ice old-timers remember him as a high scoring defenseman noted for his rink length dashes.

In addition to being named by the Minnesota Athletic Hall of Fame as the finest hockey player ever produced in the state, he was also selected to the Hockey Hall of Fame in Toronto in 1952.

Malcolm K. Gordon

St. Paul's School
(1888-1917)

Coach

Born: Jan. 10, 1868, Baltimore, Maryland

In 1882 Malcolm K. Gordon arrived as a "new kid" at the St. Paul's School in Concord, New Hampshire. He not only was an only child who knew no one else in the school, he was also a Southerner, dropped into a nest of hostile Yankees.

In one of those odd incongruities of life, this Southerner was to play a major role in shaping what is regarded as an essentially Northern game — our great sport of hockey.

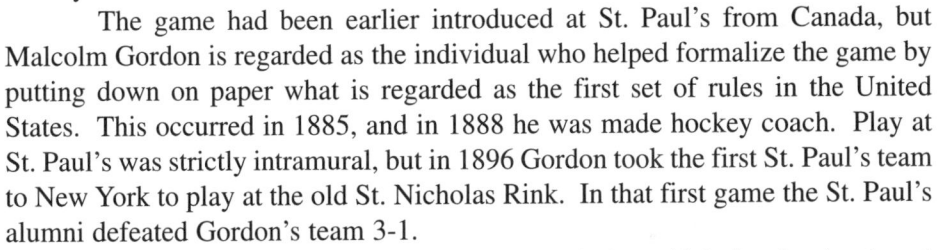

The game had been earlier introduced at St. Paul's from Canada, but Malcolm Gordon is regarded as the individual who helped formalize the game by putting down on paper what is regarded as the first set of rules in the United States. This occurred in 1885, and in 1888 he was made hockey coach. Play at St. Paul's was strictly intramural, but in 1896 Gordon took the first St. Paul's team to New York to play at the old St. Nicholas Rink. In that first game the St. Paul's alumni defeated Gordon's team 3-1.

His coaching career extended until 1917, during which time he developed numerous players, including Hobey Baker, for the Eastern colleges. It was such former players who provided the financial backing for the St. Nicholas Rink. Gordon was head of the history department at St. Paul's and in addition to hockey, also coached football and cricket as well.

After World War I service he was in the real estate business until 1927, when he founded the Malcolm K. Gordon School in Garrison, New York. He served as headmaster until his retirement in 1952, but continued to teach at the school almost to the time of his death at age 96.

Malcolm Gordon

Edward J. Jeremiah

Dartmouth College
(1937-1943 & 1945-1967)

Coach

Born: November 4, 1905, Worchester, Mass.

Eddie Jeremiah entered Dartmouth in 1926 after attending high school in Somerville, Mass., and prep school at Hebron Academy in Maine. He earned nine letters at Somerville, in football, hockey, and baseball, while earning three more in those same sports at Hebron.

Eddie Jeremiah

After picking up two football, three hockey, and two baseball letters at Dartmouth, Jeremiah entered the professional hockey ranks as a member of the New Haven hockey team of the Canadian-American League. He then split the next season between the New York Americans and the Boston Bruins of the National Hockey League. He also spent the 1933 season with both the Boston Cubs and the New Haven team, again in the Canadian-American League. His last year of playing was the 1935 season with Cleveland of the International League.

With his playing days over, he went on to become the coach of the Boston Olympics hockey team and guided them to the National Amateur Athletic Union Championship in 1936. He became varsity hockey coach at Dartmouth a year later and served continuously after that date, except for World War II service, until his retirement in 1967.

Dartmouth hockey flourished under Jeremiah. In seven of the first nine years Jeremiah was at the coaching helm, the Indians won the Pentagonal League Championship, and, from 1942-1946, the program won a record 46 consecutive games without a defeat. In addition, he led Dartmouth to the NCAA tournament in both 1948 and 1949, and captured Ivy League titles in 1959 and 1960 as well. In these decades as Dartmouth's head coach, Jeremiah directed his teams to 308 victories, 247 losses and 12 ties. He remains a Big Green coaching legend even to this day.

Michael G. Karakas

Chicago Blackhawks
(1935-1940, 1944-1946)
Montreal Canadians (1939-1940)
Goaltender
Born: December 12, 1911, Aurora, Minn.

Mike Karakas was the first of a number of players coached by enshrinee Cliff Thompson to go on to stardom in the National Hockey league. Karakas had his first hockey training on the ice in a lot near the Spruce Mine of Eveleth, where he and other sons of Oliver Iron Mining Company (now United States Steel, donators of the site of the United States Hockey Hall of Fame) fought out their hockey battles. He played hockey on the Eveleth High School team for three years, and later, while attending Eveleth Junior College, he joined the Rangers, an amateur club which won the state championship in 1931.

Karakas soon attracted the attention of a scout for the AHA's Chicago Shamrocks, where he was used as a backup goalie that year and as a regular the next. He was later named as the AHA's most valuable goalie. After trying out with the Detroit Red Wings, he was sent to St. Louis, playing there and at Tulsa for the next two years. Both St. Louis and Tulsa were members of the AHA, then hockey's top minor league.

Karakas joined the Chicago Blackhawks at the start of the 1936 season and proceeded to dazzle the opposition by posting a 1.92 goals against average and 9 shutouts over the 48-game season. This was more than sufficient to gain him the forerunner to the Calder Trophy as the league's top rookie. In 1938 Karakas backstopped the Hawks to a Stanley Cup victory despite an injury during the final series. He even recorded two shutouts during the eight playoff games. He played with the Blackhawks into the 1940 season and ended that year with the Montreal Canadiens.

Playing the next three seasons in the American Hockey League with Providence, Karakas returned to the Hawks in 1944 and took them all the way to the Stanley Cup finals against the Montreal Canadiens. Though the Blackhawks went out in four straight games, all but the first was close, and Karakas performed brilliantly.

The following season he shared the league lead in shutouts with four, and was also named as a second team All-Star. After the 1946 season Karakas returned to the Providence Reds of the American League where he finished his professional career. He is a true Eveleth hockey legend.

Thomas F. Lockhart

Amateur Hockey Association of the United States (1937-1972)

Administrator

Born: March 21, 1892, New York, NY

Thomas Lockhart's name has been synonymous with amateur hockey in the United States since the early 1930's, when he took over the organization and promotion of the game in New York City. Long interested and active as a cyclist, boxer and track competitor, he organized the Eastern Amateur Hockey League in 1933, and in the fall of 1937 founded the Amateur Hockey Association of the United States (AHAUS). The latter without a doubt has been Lockhart's greatest achievement in the world of sports.

Lockhart and other hockey enthusiasts in the United States realized hockey people were required to run the game efficiently on a nationwide basis. Until then, the sport had been under the direction of varying athletic governing bodies for various time periods. AHAUS has continued to grow and prosper over the years.

The first national youth hockey tournaments for boys under high school age was held in 1949. Presently, national tournaments in multiple classes are held annually. In the past decade youth hockey has displayed a tremendous growth in the country and at the present time the game is played in 44 of the 50 states. There are now literally hundreds of thousands of kids and tens of thousands of teams presently competing in formal programs around the country — all a tribute to Lockhart's vision.

Lockhart's other hockey endeavors have involved supervising the New York Metropolitan Amateur League, coaching and managing the New York Rovers of the Eastern Amateur League, and serving as business manager of the New York Rangers. He has also served on the United States Olympic Ice Hockey Committee and the International Ice hockey Federation. Lockhart was also selected to the Hockey Hall of Fame in Toronto in 1965.

Myles J. Lane

Dartmouth College (1924-1928)

Defenseman

Born: October 2, 1903, Melrose, Mass.

Myles Lane ranks as one of Dartmouth College's greatest all-time athletes. From 1925 until his graduation in 1928, Lane earned three letters in hockey and football, respectively, and another in baseball. He was captain of the 1928 hockey team, and led the squad to a 6-4 record.

Myles Lane

While at Dartmouth he established records for the most goals in a season by a defenseman, 20, and career goals by a defenseman, 50. Lane was also an outstanding football player at Dartmouth, starring as a halfback for three seasons. (In addition, he also received All-American recognition for his gridiron exploits and is a member of the National Football Foundation's Hall of Fame at Brunswick, New Jersey.)

As a sophomore he played on the 1925 team which was undefeated, 8-0-0, and acclaimed as national champions. In 1926, the Indians had a 4-4 record, but swept to a 7-1 mark in 1927, losing only to Yale, as Lane scored 125 of his team's 280 points.

Lane later gained national prominence by becoming the first American collegian to successfully enter the ranks of professional hockey, when he joined the New York Rangers in 1928. During his initial professional hockey season with the Rangers, Lane was sold to the Boston Bruins, where he went on to a Stanley Cup victory over the Montreal Canadiens. Lane was also a teammate of George Owen, another United States Hockey Hall of Fame enshrinee, on this club. He returned for a portion of the 1930 season, as well as for the 1934 campaign too.

Following his hockey playing days, Lane went on to pursue a career in the law, where he became one of the nation's most successful trial lawyers and foes of organized crime.

Sam L. LoPresti

Chicago Blackhawks (1940-1942)

Goaltender

Born: January 30, 1917, Elcor, Minn.

Sam LoPresti, born in Elcor but raised in Eveleth, is one of two American hockey players to have his name written into National Hockey League record book. On page 93, you'll find the category: "Most shots, one Team, One Game" followed by: 83, Boston Bruins, March 4, 1941 at Boston. Boston defeated Chicago 3-2. Chicago goaltender was Sam LoPresti." On that night in Boston, with fellow Evelethian and Hall of Famer Frank Brimsek in the opposing nets, LoPresti turned aside 27 saves in the first period, 31 in the second, and 22 in the last. After the game the late Johnny Crawford, a Bruin forward summed it up best when asked if LoPresti was really good or just lucky: "He was good all right... if he hadn't been good he wouldn't be alive now."

Another of legendary Eveleth Coach Cliff Thompson's protégé's, he took over the goalie's job in his second year out for the high school team. In 1936 LoPresti played in the nets for the Eveleth Junior College team, also coached by Cliff Thompson, and the club had one of its most successful seasons. After a year at St. Cloud Teacher's College he returned to play for the Junior College. Thompson felt he was a natural in the nets. LoPresti never got flustered when in the midst of a shower of pucks as his record breaking performance was to prove.

In the fall of 1939 the St. Paul Saints sent a scout to Eveleth to dig up some goalie talent. The scout contacted Thompson who promptly recommended LoPresti. From St. Paul, which played in the American Hockey Association, it wasn't long before he found himself in the Chicago nets when Paul Goodman retired. LoPresti played through the end of the 1942 season when he entered the U.S. Navy. There, aboard a merchant ship that was torpedoed in February of 1943, he incredibly spent 42 days in a lifeboat before being rescued.

After the war LoPresti played senior amateur hockey in Northeastern Minnesota before retiring from the game. His son, Pete, also went on to prominence as a goaltender, later starring for the hometown Minnesota North Stars in the 1970s.

John P. Mariucci

Chicago Blackhawks
(1940-1942 & 1945-1948)

Defenseman

Born: May 8, 1916, Eveleth, Minn.

The name of John Mariucci is indelibly etched into the history of American hockey as well as that of his native Minnesota. He did, in the words of an old but appropriate cliché, become a legend in his own time. Mariucci was another Cliff Thompson coached player who went on to bigger and better things. After attending high school in Eveleth he went on to the University of Minnesota, where he starred in football as well as on the ice — even leading his squad to an undefeated AAU National Championship in 1940.

Turning pro that year, Mariucci played briefly for Providence of the American League before joining the Hawks for the balance of the season. In Chicago he became a fixture manning the Blackhawks defense until the end of the 1948 season and eventually becoming the team captain in the process. Never one to back away from a fight, the hard rock Mariucci was second in penalty minutes during the 1946-47 season gathering 110 to Toronto's Gus Mortson. Before retiring after the 1951 season he played for St. Louis in the American League and Minneapolis and St. Paul in the United States League. During World War II Mariucci also played for the Coast Guard team in the Eastern Amateur League.

Returning to his alma mater as varsity hockey coach in 1952, Mariucci piloted the Gophers through the end of the 1966 season. Long a champion of the American player he stoutly maintained that the American boys were as good as his Canadian counterpart if given the opportunity. In accordance with his philosophy his teams at Minnesota were almost exclusively American in make-up. His most memorable Gopher team was the 1954 squad which went all the way to the NCAA finals before bowing to Rensselaer Polytechnic Institute, 5-4, in overtime.

Mariucci later served as Special Assistant to Lou Nanne, the General Manager of the Minnesota North Stars, where his duties ranged from coaching to scouting. He worked tirelessly throughout his life to advance the sport of hockey in the Midwest, and did more to promote the game than arguably anyone. In 1987 the hockey half of Williams Arena was renamed as Mariucci Arena in his honor. A legend, a character, an infamous brawler, and a true gentleman, Maroosh will always remain immortalized as the "Godfather of Minnesota hockey."

George Owen Jr.

Boston Bruins (1928-1933)

Defenseman

Born: December 2, 1901, Hamilton, Ontario

Shortly after his birth, George Owen's parents moved to the Boston area, where young George grew up and learned his hockey. He attended Newton High School and went on to Harvard in the fall of 1919. There, he captained the Freshman team and later served two terms as varsity captain, a relatively rare feat at Harvard. As a college hockey player, he was equally at home on defense or at center. Owen also played football and baseball for the Crimson, serving as captain of the latter during his senior year.

Following graduation, Owen entered the brokerage business and continued to play hockey with distinction for the strong Boston University Club. He was invited to play for the United States Olympic Team in 1924, but was forced to decline because of business obligations.

So strong a player was Owen, that the Boston Bruins signed him as a professional at the relatively late age of twenty-six. He played five seasons with the Bruins teaming at various times on defense with both Lionel Hitchman and Eddie Shore. Owen was also a member of the 1929 Bruins team which won the Stanley Cup.

He enjoyed his finest Stanley Cup Series in 1931 when he had two goals and three assists in a five game losing series to the Montreal Canadiens. His goal in the fourth game iced the victory for Boston. A high scoring defenseman in the days of the 44 game schedule. Owen scored 46 goals and 38 assists in five years of regular season and playoff action.

Winthrop H. "Ding" Palmer

Yale University (1927-1930)

Forward

Born: Dec. 5, 1906, Warehouse Point, Conn.

Notching 87 goals from 1927-30, Ding Palmer emerged as Yale University's all-time leading goal scorer, and even finished as the school's No. 4 all-time point producer with 96.

Palmer played on varsity squads that lost just six games in three years during that same time span. In 1928, the Elis were 13-4-0, but improved that to 15-1-1 in 1929. In addition, the 1930 team, called the "greatest amateur hockey team in history" by E.S. Bronson, was 17-1-1.

Incredibly, the teams Palmer played on posted an aggregate record of 45-6-2 during his three years. In 1930, Palmer led the nation in scoring with 27 goals, 9 assists. Playing as a left wing, Palmer scored most of his goals unassisted and loved to shoot from mid-ice. He had an astounding 41 goals in the 1928 season and got seven goals in one game against New Hampshire. During the Harvard series in his senior year, he played outstanding defensively as well as offensively. His junior season was marred by illness; plagued by the flu, he played in just about half the schedule.

After leaving Yale, Palmer played on the 1932 United States Olympic Team which garnered a silver medal at Lake Placid, and also on the 1933 National Team which won the World Championship at Prague, defeating Canada 2-1 in the epic final game.

Ding Palmer

Elwyn N. "Doc" Romnes

Chicago Blackhawks
Toronto Maple Leafs
New York Americans
(1930-1940)

Forward

Born: Jan. 1, 1907, White Bear Lake, Minn.

After starring at White Bear Lake High School, Doc Romnes went on to play his college hockey at St. Thomas University in St. Paul. Then, in 1927, after three years with the local St. Paul Saints, he broke into the National Hockey League at a time when there were but two American born players in the league. Fortunately for him the Chicago Blackhawks team which he joined got off to a bad start and Romnes got a chance at center and played regularly thereafter.

Romnes played in the Stanley Cup finals on four different occasions: 1931, 1934, 1938, all with Chicago, and 1939 with the Toronto Maple Leafs. He was a winner in 1934 with fellow enshrinee Taffy Abel and in 1938 with enshrinees Cully Dahlstrom and Mike Karakas. The saga of the 1938 team stands out particularly in Romnes' career because of his uncharacteristically violent encounter with Toronto defensemen Red Hoerner, who broke his nose in five places. Ironically both were teammates in Toronto the following year when Romnes scored the winning goal in the Leafs only victory over the Boston Bruins in the Stanley Cup finals.

Such a gentleman was Romnes, that in all of his regular-season and play-off career games, he drew just 46 penalty minutes in 403 games. Because of that, in 1936, he won the Lady Byng Trophy, scoring 13 goals and 25 assists along with tallying just six penalty minutes in the full 48 game schedule. (The Lady Byng Trophy is awarded to the player adjudged to have exhibited the best type of sportsmanship and gentlemanly conduct combined with a high standard of playing ability).

After the 1940 season Romnes retired and coached Michigan Tech until 1945. He led the Kansas City Pla Mors to the United States Hockey League Championship and Playoff Title in 1946 and then coached the University of Minnesota varsity from 1947 until 1952. He should be regarded as one of Minnesota's best-ever both on the ice and off.

Doc Romnes

Clifford R. Thompson

Eveleth High School (1926-1958)

Coach

Born: Sept. 10, 1893, Minneapolis, Minn.

Legendary coach Cliff Thompson guided Eveleth High School from 1920 until his retirement in 1958. During that time his teams won an amazing 534 games while losing only 26 and tying just nine. The highlight of Thompson's career came during the years 1948-51 when his Golden Bears won 78 straight games, including four straight Minnesota state high school hockey championships. Eveleth won the state title a total of five times under Thompson's leadership.

Cliff Thompson

Simultaneous to his high school coaching, Thompson also handled the Eveleth Junior College team compiling a career record of 171 games won and 28 lost. In fact, his Junior College squad even garnered the nation's top collegiate ranking on several occasions during the late 1920s, even beating out the likes of Minnesota, Michigan and Yale.

Generations of Eveleth youngsters received hockey instructions from Cliff Thompson, and in addition to his giving them the best hockey leadership, he was the object of deep affection that only boys can have for a man as close to them as their coach and teacher. Many stories are told how Thompson helped dozens of youngsters get a good pair of skates during the depression. And when it came to equipment for his players he was a stickler for the very best available. Eveleth's claim to hockey fame can be traced to Cliff Thompson's efforts in player development. No less than 11 Eveleth players went on to perform in the National Hockey League and virtually all of them learned the game from Thompson. Foremost among them were Frank Brimsek, Mike Karakas, Sam LoPresti, and John Mariucci — all Hall of Famers. Other outstanding Thompson-developed players who went on to college and National/Olympic Team stardom were John Mayasich, John Matchefts and Willard Ikola, who are also each in the Hall of Fame as well.

Thompson was honored in 1951 with a trophy dedication at the Minneapolis Sportsman's Show for his coaching record and efforts in training hockey players in good citizenship as well as athletics. He was made an honorary member of the American Hockey Coaches Association in 1957, one of only a handful of men ever so honored.

William Thayer Tutt

International Ice Hockey Federation (1959-1973)

Administrator

Born: March 2, 1912, Coronado, Calif.

William Thayer Tutt of Colorado Springs, Colorado is president of the El Pomar Foundation and the Broadmoor Hotel, Inc. and its related companies. It has been serving in these capacities that Tutt has exercised his administrative abilities in hockey.

Thayer Tutt

During the 1948 college season, a group of coaches, including Vic Heyliger, then of Michigan, approached Tutt concerning the sponsorship of a National Collegiate Athletic Association (NCAA) hockey tournament. Tutt agreed to provide his backing and thus college hockey was launched as a truly national sport. The tournament was held at the Broadmoor Hotel from 1948 through 1957, returning there in 1969 for a one year stand. Since 1958 the tournament has been moved around the country to various college hockey hotbeds.

Thayer Tutt is generally regarded as the "Father of the NCAA Hockey Tournament" for his pioneering work for the college game. Turning his attention to international hockey Tutt has also been a member or President of the United States International Ice Hockey Federation since 1959. This period was characterized by the increasing visibility of the international game which was brought to a dramatic forefront by the Russia-Team Canada series in September 1972.

Long interested in youth hockey in this country Tutt succeeded his long time friend, Tom Lockhart, also a United States Hockey Hall of Fame enshrinee, as President of the Amateur Hockey Association of the United States in June 1972. Tutt went on to serve as the North American Vice President of the International Ice Hockey Federation and also served on the U.S. Olympic Committee. In addition, he is also involved with the National Cowboy Hall of Fame, golf, and figure skating.

Alfred "Ralph" Winsor

Harvard University (1902-1917)

Coach

Born: 1881, Brookline, Mass.

The dominating figure of the first 20 years of Harvard hockey was without question Ralph Winsor. The early period of Harvard hockey might very well be called the "Winsor Era." He starred for the Crimson during the early 1900s and even captained the 1902 team. Then he coached with outstanding success from 1902 to 1917, during which time Harvard had 124 wins and 29 defeats. The teams of 1903, 1904, 1905, 1906, 1909 and 1919, when he was assistant coach, were undefeated.

Ralph Winsor

Over these years he also compiled a 23-5 win-loss record against arch rival Yale. As might be expected Winsor developed many stars. Foremost among them was S. Trafford Hicks, Class of 1910, and captain of the 1910 team. Another was Morgan B. Phillips, Class of 1915, who tallied nine goals in games against the Eli.

Winsor was an innovator who took part in the development of the modern hockey stick and shoe skates, as well as computing and adopting the official radii for the blades, known for years as the "Harvard Radius." Many new tactics, such as back-checking, and the shift of defensemen from point and cover point to the present paring positions are credited to Winsor's genius as well.

In all those years it is reported that Winsor never took any money for his coaching duties, and his great modesty kept him from appearing in any team pictures. Besides his great contribution at Harvard, Winsor aided hockey at the schoolboy level and at other colleges.

He also had the distinction of coaching the United States Olympic Team at the 1932 games at Lake Placid, losing only once 2-1, to Canada in the final game. Fellow United States Hockey Hall of Fame enshrines John Chase, John Garrison, and Ding Palmer were all members of that 1932 team.

Frank J. "Coddy" Winters

Cleveland Crescents
Cleveland Athletic Club
1908-1925

Forward-Defenseman

Born: January 29, 1884, Duluth, Minn.

Frank "Coddy" Winters started out as an ice polo player in his home town of Duluth back in the late 1800s. As ice polo gave way to hockey, however, Winters took up the game as a rover — where his great speed could be utilized to the best advantage. Winters played with the Duluth Northern Hardware team through the 1908 season, during which the team played a series of games with a Cleveland All-Stars at the new Elysium Rink. Winters starred in the series and fell in love with Cleveland. That summer he moved there and played the rest of his career for various Cleveland amateur teams.

From 1909-11, Winters played at rover and then switched to defense in 1912. There he proved to be just as good in checking opponents as he had been in carrying the puck down the ice. During Winters' 17-year career in Cleveland he played on three championship teams: 1912, 1914, and 1922.

Winters' had tremendous speed and contemporary accounts of games he played in recount this vividly: "Coddy rushed the chunk of rubber up and down the ice and across the back with his old daring and recklessness and he hurdled and twisted with small ceremony although with much éclat."

While playing in Cleveland Winters coached the Case Tech teams and made several trips to Philadelphia to coach the University of Pennsylvania team as well. Though having the opportunity to turn professional, he preferred to remain an amateur. There were many who felt Winters was equal in talent to Hobey Baker, also an enshrinee of the United States Hockey Hall of Fame, who many regard as one of the greatest American bred hockey players. Following his retirement from the game Winters remained in Cleveland working in the sporting goods business.

Lyle Z. Wright

Minneapolis Arena (1924-1963)
Minneapolis Millers (1928-31)

Manager/Administrator

Born: Sept. 28, 1898, Winnipeg, Canada

Lyle Wright was identified with organized hockey from the first moment it existed in Minneapolis and remained identified with it, in one capacity or another, until his death. Wright served in the Canadian artillery in World War I and moved to Minneapolis in 1919.

After four years of playing hockey, he brought the famed Ching Johnson from Eveleth to Minneapolis to play for the Minneapolis Millers. He managed the Millers, who played in the American Hockey Association, from 1928 until 1931, and then moved to Chicago to become business manager of the Blackhawks. He returned to Minneapolis in the early 1930's and remained there for the remainder of his life serving in varying capacities with the Minneapolis Arena eventually attaining the office of the president.

Over the years of his affiliation with the Minneapolis Arena, he was involved with the minor-league professional Minneapolis Millers almost continuously during their existence. But the Millers were not his only hockey interest. It was at the Arena that University of Minnesota hockey got its start, justifying the construction of a hockey arena on campus. It was also at the Arena that through Wright's cooperation high school hockey flourished to become a major high school sport.

Wright's friends described him as a "practical promoter, a man with bold ideas, and a skilled organizer." In hockey he was an advocate of more scoring, less padding for goalies, and the determination that Minneapolis was a major league town. He was instrumental in bringing the Millers such hockey greats as Tiny Thompson, Stew Adams, and United States Hockey Hall of Fame enshrinee Taffy Abel. In addition to hockey, Wright was also involved in figure skating, the Ice Follies, and the Minneapolis Aquatennial.

THE CLASS OF 1974

William L. "Bill" Chadwick

National Hockey League Referee (1940-1955)

Born: October 10, 1915, New York, NY

Bill Chadwick rose from the relatively unlikely hockey background of New York City to become one of the premier referees to officiate in the National Hockey League. When he laid his whistle aside after the 1955 season he was the senior official in the NHL, the only American to ever achieve that position.

Chadwick was a protégé and long time friend of United States Hockey Hall of Fame enshrinee Tom Lockhart, President of the Amateur Hockey Association of the United States from 1937 to 1972. He played his early hockey with the Stock Exchange team in the New York Metropolitan League. This League usually played preliminary games before the New York Rovers traditional Sunday afternoon games in Madison Square Garden. It was while playing in the Metro League that he caught the eye of a scout and won a spot on the Rover's team. Then, it was while sitting out a Rovers game because of an injury that Chadwick got his first officiating opportunity. Encouraged by Lockhart, he took an immediate liking to this aspect of the game and was soon working numerous amateur games in the New York area. An NHL official observed his work and Chadwick spent the 1940 season as a linesman before becoming a referee.

Similar to another United States Hockey Hall of Fame enshrinee, Ralph Winsor, Chadwick was a hockey innovator. Not knowing what to do with his hands he developed the signals now in common use for denoting penalties. While the initial reaction to Chadwick clasping his wrist for a holding penalty was negative, it soon became apparent that he had introduced a desirable feature to the game for all concerned. Hand signals quickly became universally used throughout the hockey world. Upon retiring Chadwick maintained an active interest in the game and later served as a color commentator for New York Ranger telecasts.

Bill Chadwick

Raymond C. Chaisson

Boston College (1939-1941)

Forward

Born: June 23, 1918, Cambridge, Mass.

Ray Chaisson centered one of the all time great lines in the history of college hockey at Boston College, along with Al Dumond and John Pryor. His coach and fellow United States Hockey Hall of Fame enshrinee, the legendary John "Snooks" Kelley, described Chaisson as one of his very finest hockey players during his 36 years of college coaching.

Ray Chaisson

The Cambridge native led the East in scoring in both the 1940 and 1941 seasons in which the Eagles posted 12-5-1 and 13-1-0 records, respectively. Chaisson's point totals those years were 67 and 59 over that same time frame as well. In a 1939 win over Cornell he had five goals in one game and 33 for the season, which was only 18 games in length.

Chaisson is the all time Boston College leader in average goals per game per season with 2.07, during the 1941 season in which he scored 29 goals over a 14-game schedule. His 126 points ranks him among the Eagles all-time career point leaders despite the fact that each of the players listed above him played in more that twice as many as the 32 games Chaisson played in. In addition, he played just two seasons in a career cut short by World War II. His eight hat tricks are still a school record.

After World War II service with the Navy, he later played senior amateur hockey with Los Angeles Monarchs of the Pacific Coast Hockey League, where he led the league in scoring with 101 points for the 1946 season. Chaisson retired from active competition after the 1947 season and went on to pursue a career in the publishing industry.

Victor Desjardins

Chicago Blackhawks
New York Rangers
Minor and Professional Teams
(1926-1938)

Forward

Born: July 4, 1900, Sault Ste. Marie, Mich.

Vic Des Jardins

Sault Ste. Marie's Vic Desjardins played a key role in the early days of Eveleth hockey when the town was represented in the United States Amateur Hockey Association (USAHA). At that time there was no professional hockey in the United States and the USAHA represented the highest level of the game in the nation.

An early writer said of him: "Desjardins of Eveleth, while one of the very smallest centers (5'9, 160 lbs.) in the game, he is one of the very smartest and is very capable on offense and defense." Backing up that comment is an excerpt from another writer who wrote: "Eveleth's winning tally was the result of the alertness of Vic Desjardins. He watched carefully for the rebound on Ching Johnson's shot and when he placed the puck it went squarely into the net."

Desjardins' knack of finding the net served him well and he entered into professional hockey with St. Paul of the American Hockey Association. In 1928 he captured the league scoring title with 20 goals and eight assists. That performance was followed by a second place finish in the 1930 scoring race with 25 goals and 10 assists, also with St. Paul.

Desjardins' scoring abilities led him to the National Hockey League with the Chicago Blackhawks for the 1931 season. There, he was a teammate of his fellow United States Hockey Hall of Fame enshrinee and Soo native, Taffy Abel, as the Hawks went all the way to the Stanley Cup Finals before losing to the Montreal Canadiens three games to two. Though scoreless in the finals, Des Jardins logged three goals and 12 assists over the regular season. Performing for the New York Rangers the following year he once again was in the finals against the Toronto Maple Leafs, this time losing three games to none.

Desjardins closed out his professional hockey career with six more years in the American Hockey Association with Tulsa and Kansas City. The highlight of these later years was a second place finish in the 1934 scoring race with 18 goals and 15 assists with Tulsa.

Doug Everett

Dartmouth College (1922-1926)

Forward

Born: April 3, 1905, Cambridge, Mass.

Doug Everett was, along with his fellow United States Hockey Hall of Fame enshrinee Myles Lane, one of the great players to come out of Dartmouth during the 1920's. He played his first hockey for Colby Academy in 1922, serving as captain of that team as well. Later he amazed fans with his stick handling ability, speed, and hard shot as a member of Dartmouth teams from 1922-1926.

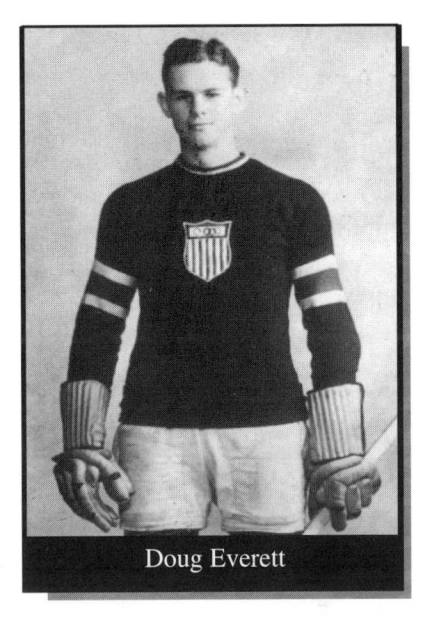

Doug Everett

Everett was All-College in his sophomore and junior years at Dartmouth, as selected by the Boston Transcript, and was named by the New York Herald Tribune to one of the earliest All-American Teams. A writer of that time said of him: "He could skate, and he could shoot, and he had the native intelligence — all the ingredients a player needs for greatness. He was hardly of the ruffian variety, but he knew how to body check and did so with authority."

After graduation Everett declined offers from the Boston Bruins, New York Rangers, and Toronto Maple Leafs to enter the insurance business. However, he continued in hockey with the University Club of Boston, playing with another United States Hockey Hall of Famer George Owens. While skating with the University Club against Princeton he even recorded six goals.

Still later, Everett played with the 1932 United States Olympic Team which finished second to Canada at Lake Placid, NY. In the Olympic tournament the United States tied Canada 2-2 in the first game and lost the second, 2-1. The former Big Green skater scored two of the three American goals in the two games. Everett was the fourth member of the 1932 Olympic Team to be enshrined in the United States Hockey Hall of Fame. Ding Palmer, John Chase, and John Garrison have already been accorded the honor.

Everett, who later had a rink named after him in Concord, New Hampshire, went on to become the Chairman of the Board of Morrill and Everett, Insurance Inc. — the same firm that he originally joined after leaving graduating from Dartmouth.

Victor Heyliger

University of Illinois (1939-43)
University of Michigan (1944-1957)
U.S. Air Force Academy (1966-1974)

Coach

Born: Sept. 26, 1915, Concord, Mass.

Vic Heyliger, with his ever present cigar clenched between his teeth, came out of the East to forge an outstanding coaching record at his alma mater, Michigan, as well as at the University of Illinois and the United States Air Force Academy.

Vic Heyliger

The stocky, black-haired coach played high school hockey at Concord and prep school hockey at the Lawrence Academy in Groton, Connecticut. Entering Michigan in 1934, he starred for the Wolverines through in 1937, later earning All-American honors at forward. He also scored a school record 116 goals as well. Following graduation in 1937, Heyliger played for the Chicago Blackhawks in 1938 and 1944 while sandwiching in a coaching stint at Illinois in the intervening years.

With the Blackhawks Heyliger alternated at left wing and center with Johnny Gottselig, who later coached the Chicago team. He attributed his own development as a coach to the teachings of former Blackhawk coaches Bill Stewart and Paul Thompson.

Heyliger's greatest years were at Michigan. Starting with the first NCAA Championships ever staged in 1948, at Colorado Springs, the Wolverines went on to capture six national titles. Dartmouth fell 8-4 that year to be followed by Boston College in 1951, Colorado College in 1952, and Minnesota in 1953. The later victory was particularly noteworthy as the Gophers had defeated the Wolverines in three of the four regular season meetings. The year of 1955 saw Michigan oppose Colorado College in the final and take home a 5-3 victory. Heyliger's sixth and final national title followed the next year with a thrilling 2-1 overtime victory over St. Lawrence, when Michigan's Tom Rendall scored from the face-off.

Among the outstanding American players coached by Heyliger at Michigan were Eveleth, Minn. natives John Matchefts and Willard Ikola, who both helped lead the United States to a silver medal victory in the 1950 Olympics. After a period of retirement Heyliger became coach at the United States Air Force Academy, guiding that relatively new hockey program through its early years before retiring at the close of the 1974 season.

Virgil Johnson

Chicago Blackhawks (1933-1947)
Minor professional teams

Defenseman

Born: March 14, 1912, Minneapolis, Minn.

Virgil Johnson came out of Minneapolis South High School where he starred in both hockey and football as a defenseman and quarterback, respectively. The ice is where he would make his mark though, as he went on to play 16 years of professional hockey.

Johnson was small in stature at five-foot-eight and 160 lbs., but nonetheless was a master stick checker and backwards skater who could take the puck away from anyone. Fellow United States Hockey Hall of Fame enshrinee John Mariucci, remembered him well: "He was one of the smallest defenseman in the league, but very effective. He was a magician with his stick. He was like a terrier after a rat when he moved in and stole the puck. He could do it against the best stick handlers."

After playing amateur hockey in the Twin Cities area, Johnson spent a large part of his career with the St. Paul Saints of the American Hockey Association. However, during the 1938 season he was called up to play with the Chicago Blackhawks for their Cinderella season. The Blackhawks took it all that year as Johnson appeared in seven of the Stanley Cup games.

He did not return to the National Hockey League until the 1944 season though, when he played the entire schedule as well as nine Stanley Cup games as the Hawks bowed to Montreal in four straight games in the finals. (In two NHL seasons, Johnson played with four United States Hockey Hall of Fame enshrinees: Karakas, Romnes, Dahlstrom, and Purpur.) After the 1947 season with the Minneapolis Millers of the United States League, he retired from professional hockey to pursue business interests in the Twin Cities.

John H. "Jack" Kelley

Colby College (1955-62)
Boston University (1962-1972)
Hartford Whalers (1972-82)
Pittsburgh Penguins (1993-Present)

Coach

Born: July 10, 1927, Medford Mass.

Jack Kelley coached Boston University to NCAA championships in 1971 and 1972, while taking the Terriers to four NCAA tournaments altogether over a 10-year span. At the professional level, his Hartford Whalers teams in the professional World Hockey Association were East Division champions three times and won the AVCO Cup playoff title in 1973.

While his coaching exploits at Boston University and Colby College, and later at Hartford, gained fame for Jack Kelley, he had earlier been an outstanding hockey player. In 1945, at Belmont High School, he was named the top Boston schoolboy performer. In 1949, Kelley competed on an AHAUS team and went to Boston University, leading the Terriers to the NCAA finals in 1950 and 1951. He was also named their most valuable player and all-ECAC in 1952.

Kelley began his coaching career at Weston High School, where he handled football, baseball, and hockey. From 1955 to 1962, he guided Colby College to the upper echelon of ECAC hockey. The lure of coaching his alma mater brought Kelley back to BU in 1962, and in addition to their national success, his teams won six Beanpot Tournament titles.

"We were about half Canadians in those days, but we had a lot of great players and some balanced teams," Kelley recollected. When the rebel WHA organized, Kelley formed the Whalers franchise and helped U.S. and collegiate players obtain professional opportunities. Kelley's overall college coaching record was 303-147-13 and his pro record 77-55-6.

He later worked for the Detroit Red Wings, running their affiliate at Glens Falls, N.Y. In 1993, he was hired as president of the Pittsburgh Penguins. Kelley and his wife, Virginia, have three sons and a daughter.

William C. Moe

New York Rangers (1944-1949)

Defenseman

Born: October 2, 1916, Danvers, Mass.

Bill Moe, like fellow enshrinee Vic Heyliger, was one of those relatively unique hockey people who shared the hockey heritage of both the East and West.

Born in Danvers, Mass., Moe grew up in Minneapolis, where he was attracted to the ice game. After playing in local amateur leagues and then with the amateur Eastern League Baltimore Orioles, he hooked on with the professional American Hockey League Philadelphia Rockets, later moving on to the Hershey Bears of the same league. He gained laurels as the most valuable player in the American League for the 1944 season and attracted the notice of Lester Patrick of the Rangers, who gave up four players to obtain his services.

Employing a unique crouching method of stopping on-rushing forwards, Moe acquired the label of the "best blocking back in hockey." In fact, he was often queried by newspaper men about whether he ever played football. Moe usually replied that he considered that game "too tough," whereupon he then scooted off to the much rougher atmosphere of the hockey rink. Actually, the tough backliner was too small as a high school boy to play football. His playing weight was only 175 lbs., not particularly big for a body checking defenseman.

Moe played for the New York Rangers at a time when there were only two other Americans playing in the National Hockey League, Frank Brimsek and John Mariucci, both United States Hockey Hall of Fame enshrinees. He fared well in the NHL, but an untimely fractured vertebra limited his Stanley Cup playoff appearances to just one game. He played for five seasons in the NHL, then returned to Hershey from 1949-51, only to play two more minor league seasons before retiring after the 1953 campaign.

Bill Moe

Clifford J. "Fido" Purpur

St. Louis Eagles (1934-35)
St. Louis Flyers (1935-42)
Chicago Blackhawks (1942-1945)
Detroit Red Wings (1945)
St. Paul Saints (1946-47)

Forward

Born: Sept. 26, 1914, Grand Forks, ND.

Fido Purpur

When Fido Purpur stepped on the ice with the St. Louis Eagles in 1934 he had become North Dakota's first native son to play in the National Hockey League. Purpur made the NHL when he was just 20 years-old and when the Eagles folded after 1935 season he signed with the American Hockey Association's St. Louis Flyers. He stayed with the Flyers until 1942 when he returned to the NHL with the Chicago Blackhawks.

In St. Louis, Purpur was idolized by the fans not only for his gutsy play, great speed and small stature, but also because he always took time out to talk to the fans and sign autographs for the youngsters. His best year of many good years in St. Louis was 1939, when he scored 35 goals and 43 assists in the regular season and three goals and three assists in the playoffs as St. Louis won the Harry F. Sinclair Trophy, which was emblematic of the league championship.

The Blackhawks obtained Purpur with the idea of teaming him on a line with Max and Doug Bentley. He was also the player they used to shadow the great Montreal player, the legendary Maurice "Rocket" Richard.

"I followed him everywhere," recalled Purpur. Playing all 50 games for the 1943 Blackhawks he scored 13 goals and 16 assists. The following year the Hawks made the Stanley Cup finals losing to Montreal 4 games to 0, but in the semifinals, Purpur had a strong series against Detroit scoring a goal in the fourth game of the five-game series. He played with both Chicago and Detroit in 1945, appearing with the later in the finals against Toronto.

Completing his professional career with St. Paul of the United States Hockey League in 1947, Purpur returned to North Dakota where he served as the coach at the University of North Dakota from 1949 to 1956. As a resident of Grand Forks, Fido was also the father of six hockey playing sons.

THE CLASS OF 1975

Anthony "Tony" Conroy

St. Paul Athletic Club
St. Paul Saints
(1915-1929)

Forward

Born: October 19, 1895, St. Paul, Minn.

Tony Conroy was part of the great St. Paul hockey tradition that is so entwined with the names of Goheen, Fitzgerald, and Weidenborner. He starred with these men through the glory years of the St. Paul Athletic Club and later with the professional St. Paul Saints of the American Hockey Association. After attending Mechanic Arts High School, he went on to play at St. Thomas College. While still in high school the young Conroy even played with the old semi-pro St. Paul Phoenix septet.

Joining the Athletic Club team, the St. Paul skater helped his club win the McNaughton Trophy, symbolic of American amateur hockey supremacy, in 1917. The team then played Lachine, Quebec, for the Ross Cup International Championship and won 7-6, despite having to play six-man hockey for the first time. After W.W.I service, Conroy returned to the Athletic Club and was one of four members of that club to make the 1920 United States Olympic Team. The U.S. finished second to Canada, losing 2-0 to the Maple Leaf skaters for their only defeat. Conroy had a strong Olympics and scored 10 goals in a 29-0 rout of Switzerland.

The speedy back-checker played great hockey for the St. Paul club in the 1920s as they were always strong contenders for the national amateur title. The team was Western champs in 1922 and again in 1923, losing both times to Boston in the national finals. The team eventually became professional and Conroy received NHL offers, but preferred to remain in St. Paul.

Tony Conroy

Francis "Austie" Harding Jr.

Harvard University (1935-1939)

Forward

Born: Sept. 26, 1917, Boston, Mass.

Austie Harding followed quickly at Harvard on the heels of his fellow Noble and Greenough graduate, Fred Moseley, and soon established his own niche as an all time Crimson ice great. Harding also played four varsity years at prep school and then captained the Harvard freshmen.

Austie Harding

Then began three outstanding varsity years during which he led the squad in scoring each year with 30, 25, and 30 point efforts, respectively. The Boston born skater's abilities were recognized early in his college career when hockey writer Irving Burwell wrote in March, 1937: "Harvard's forward line against Yale will have Harding, without question the best American college hockey player of today at center."

Harvard captured the Ivy League title during Harding's first varsity year, 1937, and was a strong contender in the next two years. During his senior year he was team captain, named an All-American, and was awarded the John Tudor Memorial Cup as the most valuable player. One of the most memorable feats of Harding's career was his last game when he played 58 of the game's 60 minutes and scored four goals and three assists in a 7-4 victory.

Certainly a true reflection of a contemporary's description of him: "A tireless easy skater and a fine stick handler." The Cambridge player attracted pro scouts, but World War II broke upon the scene precluding any venture in this direction. Returning from war time service Harding concluded his hockey playing with the Boston Athletic Association.

He was later honored by being named to reknowned hockey historian S. Kip Farrington's 1921-45 Harvard era team as a center.

Stewart Iglehart

Yale University
Crescent Athletic Club
New York Rovers
(1929-1936)

Defenseman

Born: Feb. 22, 1910, Valparaiso, Chile

Stewart Iglehart occupies a unique position in American sports being the only man to have represented the United States internationally in two sports: hockey on the 1933 World Championship Team and polo in the 1936 International Match. He has been one of only a handful of men in polo to earn a ten goal rating. but as he says himself: "I have played many sports, some better than others, but hockey was always number one. I felt it gave me wings, an extra dimension and when I dream dreams of past accomplishments, let me dream in hockey."

As a youngster Iglehart was introduced to hockey by C.C. Pell, a former Harvard great, who taught him the rudiments of the game with an emphasis on building legs and deception in movement using the shoulders and eyes. He went on to play at the St. Paul's School, a great breeding ground of American hockey which also produced fellow enshrinees Malcolm Gordon and Hobey Baker.

The Chilean born star then went on to play varsity hockey at Yale from 1928-32, leading his '31 team to a championship. During his undergraduate days he was regarded as one of the outstanding defensemen developed in the college game. Selected to both the 1932 and 1936 Olympic Teams, Iglehart was unable to play due to varying conflicting responsibilities. He did, however, perform brilliantly for the 1933 United States world champions not only on defense, but at right wing and center.

Returning from world tournament play Iglehart played with the Crescent Athletic Club which eventually became the New York Rovers. The team was an outstanding collection of future NHL talent with such names as Colville, Shebicky, and Patrick dotting the roster. Iglehart more than held his own in this competition and most hockey observers of the day felt he could easily have moved up to the New York Rangers with the others. Instead he preferred to continue his business career on a full-time basis. He concluded his hockey playing days with the legendary St. Nicholas Hockey Club of New York City.

Stewart Iglehart

Joseph C. Linder

Portage Lake Hockey Club
Hancock Hockey Club
Shamrock Hockey Club
Duluth Curling Club
Duluth Hockey Club
(1904-1920)

Forward-Defenseman

Born: Aug. 12, 1886, Hancock, Mich.

Joe Linder

Joe Linder was described by contemporaries and those who have made a study of the game as the "first great American-born hockey player." A powerful raw-boned, virtually irresistible skater, playmaker and team leader, Linder was involved in the American hockey scene as an amateur and professional player from 1904-1920. From then until his death in 1948, he remained on the scene as a coach, manager and sponsor of the game in the Superior-Duluth area. During his Hancock High School years, 1901-04, Linder participated in and starred in hockey, baseball and football, even captaining all three sports every year of his career.

In 1904, as a high school senior, he was selected by Doc Gibson, a charter United States Hockey Hall of Fame enshrinee, to play on the Portage Lake Michigan hockey teams in league and championship play. Following a brief stay in the professional ranks, Linder returned to amateur hockey from 1905-11, playing in the Copper Country in the upper peninsula of Michigan.

He later took a team into the new American Amateur Hockey Association playing out of Duluth from 1912-20. The Linder-captained team reached its greatest heights on March 7, 1914, when they defeated the famous Victoria's of Winnipeg for what proved to be the first victory of an American team over the Canadian champs. In the game write-up a sports reporter said, "Capt. Joe Linder played like a veritable demon. On offense and defense Linder stood out as one of the greatest men I have ever seen on ice."

Shortly after his retirement as an active player, Linder entered the grocery business in Superior, Wisconsin. He remained active in the "Head of the Lakes" business and sports community in his later years. A few years before his death he was honored in the February, 1941 issue of Esquire when, in a review of the American and Canadian hockey scene, it was stated that "any list of the 30 best hockey players the whole world has had, would have to include the American-born Linder."

Frederick R. Moseley, Jr.

Harvard University (1932-1936)

Forward

Born: July 13, 1913, Brookline, Mass.

His fellow United States Hockey Hall of Fame enshrinee John Chase has perhaps best summed up Fred Moseley, as a hockey player: "Throughout his hockey career he was a tremendous team player...a tireless, powerful skater, a great back checker, and a leader on and off the ice."

Fred Mosely

Like many great Eastern hockey players, Moseley followed the traditional prep school path to the ice game. A Noble and Greenough graduate, Fred Moseley moved on to Harvard, where he immediately became a regular on the freshman team. After that, there was never any doubt as to who would be the center ice man for the Crimson over the next three years. Moseley went on to captain the 1936 team, which captured the school's first Ivy League title with a 5-1 record.

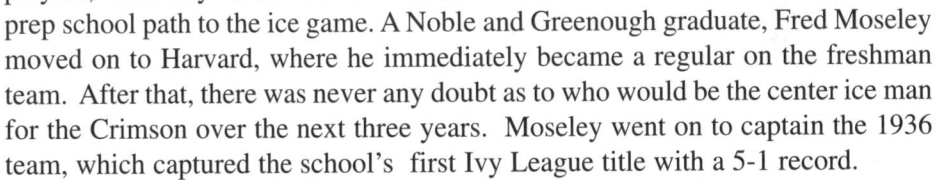

Overall the team posted a 14-4-2 record. (The Ivy League for hockey did not formally start until the 1934 season.) Named an All-American that year, Moseley added this honor to his capture of the John Tudor Memorial Cup the prior season. (The Tudor Cup is given annually to the most valuable member of the Harvard hockey team who displays ability, sportsmanship, leadership, team cooperation, and what John Tudon, '29, called "the old come through in the pinch.") The trophy was established following the 1930 season by members of the Porcelain club who were classmates of Tudor, captain of the 1929 hockey team.

Moseley also competed in football and baseball for Harvard, but it is in hockey where he left his mark at the school being named to Harvard's hall of fame for the sport. In addition, legendary hockey historian S. Kip Farrington named him to his all Harvard team for the 1921-45 period. Moseley closed his hockey career through service with the St. Nicholas squad and later with the Beaver Dam club in the Winter Club League.

THE CLASS OF 1976

William "Bill" Cleary

Harvard University (1952-1956)
United States National and Olympic Teams (1956-1960)

Forward

Born: August 19, 1934, Cambridge, Mass.

Bill Cleary etched his name permanently in the annual of American hockey history through his brilliant scoring efforts in the 1960 United States gold medal victory at Squaw Valley. Cleary's 12 points on six goals and six assists was tops on the U.S. squad and his early goal against the Russians set the tone for the epic 2-1 upset win.

Cleary's rise to stardom began well before Squaw Valley though. A product of the New England prep school tradition, in his case Belmont Hill, the Cambridge skater went on to a standout career at Harvard. Such Crimson records as most goals in a season, 42; most points in a season, 89; and most assists in a game, 8, belonged to him at the time of his graduation in 1956. Cleary captured the coveted John Tudor Cup, an MVP type award, for the 1955 season when he led the Crimson to a 17-3-1 record, the Beanpot and Ivy League championships; and a third-place finish at the NCAA tournament. Establishing a then-NCAA single season record of 89 points, Cleary was selected for All Ivy, All East, and All American honors as well as being named the most valuable player in New England.

Following his college career, Cleary continued in hockey, playing on three other Olympic/National teams in addition to the 1960 squad. Then, in March of 1971, Cleary took over the Harvard coaching reins upon "Cooney" Weiland's retirement. He had handled the freshman since 1968 and was Weiland's assistant since 1970. During the intervening years Harvard reached the NCAA tournament on several occasions.

Bill Cleary

John Mayasich

University of Minnesota (1951-1955)
U.S. Olympic/National Teams (1956-1969)

Forward-Defenseman

Born: May 22, 1933, Eveleth, Minn.

"Mayasich, who was probably the best amateur hockey player in America at the time, added muscle and hustle to the defense...," so said Coach Jack Riley, speaking of the Eveleth born and reared skater whose addition to the 1960 U.S. Olympic Team helped bring this country its first gold medal.

A product of the Hall of Fame's native city, Mayasich has long been regarded as one of the finest amateur hockey players over produced in the United States. From the days when he led Eveleth High School to four straight undefeated seasons as a perennial state high school champion (1948-1951), his name was linked with hockey.

After playing for coaching legend Cliff Thompson in Eveleth, Mayasich went on to play for another Eveleth coaching legend, John Mariucci, at the University of Minnesota — both of whom are also U.S. Hockey Hall of Fame enshrinees. The silky smooth skater went on to three great years at Minnesota, being named an All American in each year — 1953-55. Minnesota made it to the NCAA Tournament in 1954, only to lose an overtime heart-breaker to R.P.I. in the championship game. The Gophers lost, but Mayasich scored four goals and five assists in two tournament games as well as being named to the all-tournament first team.

His 29-49-78 and 41-39-80 scoring logs were good enough to win WCHA scoring titles in 1954 and 1955 as well. Following college, Mayasich was a performer with eight U.S. Olympic and National teams beginning with the 1956 silver medal winner.

It is, of course, the 1960 team which is so well remembered though. Mayasich, who had by this time been shifted to defense, played brilliantly. His slap shot at Canadian goalie Don Head was quickly converted for a goal which proved to be the winner in the critical 2-1 victory. Declining professional hockey opportunities, Mayasich devoted his remaining hockey career to the amateur Green Bay Bobcats.

Mayasich, who owns nearly every major scoring record at both the high school level, and also at the University of Minnesota, went on to become an executive with a Twin Cities radio and television station.

Robert B. Ridder

U.S. Olympic/National Teams (1952, 1956)
Minn. Amateur Hockey Assoc. (1947-1960)

Administrator

Born: July 21, 1919, New York, NY.

Bob Ridder

Among those who have made Minnesota a leader in the sport of hockey throughout the United States stands the name of Bob Ridder. Ridder, a native New Yorker and Harvard University graduate, began his hockey involvement with the Duluth Heralds, a senior amateur team at the 1940's. This interest then led to a belief that a state organization for all levels of amateur hockey was essential in Minnesota. Thus, in October of 1947 he, along with fellow enshrinee Don Clark, and Everett "Buck" Riley, founded the Minnesota Amateur Hockey Association (MAHA).

The organization, now simply called "Minnesota Hockey," ranks as one of the leading amateur associations in the world, consistently producing among the most registered players in North America.

By 1952 Ridder's interests had expanded to international hockey, and with Eveleth born Connie Pleban, he managed the 1952 United States Olympic Team. Under his dynamic leadership the team was successfully organized and financed. In Olympic competition the United States made a very formidable showing, finishing in second place, just one game behind the eventual champions from Canada.

Ridder again managed the 1956 U.S. entry which was coached by United States Hockey Hall of Fame enshrinee John Mariucci. This team also won a silver medal with a well deserved 4-1 victory over Canada as the highlight. When professional hockey came to Minnesota in 1966, Ridder became one of the nine North Star owners.

He later served as a United States Hockey Hall of Fame director, and remained active in promoting the game of hockey for both men and women throughout his life. An extremely successful businessman, Ridder was truly a man who made a difference in the world of hockey.

THE CLASS OF 1977

Earl F. Bartholome

Minneapolis Millers (1932-1935), Rochester Mustangs (1935-1936), Cleveland Barons (1936-1946), Minneapolis Millers, (1946-1950)

Forward

Born: June 21, 1913, Valley City, ND.

Earl Bartholome went on to star at Minneapolis West High School, where he played on three consecutive high school championship teams from 1929-31. After a stint with the Flour City amateurs, Bartholome turned pro with the Minneapolis Millers. From there he went to Rochester, of the then International League, for one season before spending the next decade with the American Hockey League's Cleveland Barons. It was at Cleveland that his greatest mark on the game was made. A center, he was a deft stick handler, smart skater, accurate shooter, and expert back checker. His most outstanding seasons were 1944 and 1945, when he finished sixth and fifth in the AHL scoring race with 67 and 81 points respectively. During his stay with the Barons the club captured the Calder Cup championship trophy on three occasions.

Bartholome is the only American born professional to appear in more than 500 games with one team. An example of his adeptness on ice is this extract from a press account of an early Millers game.

"There was a scrimmage beyond the Hibbing blue line when the rookie center, alert to any opportunity, hooked the puck from the mass of players, cleared out and then skated prettily and unmolested toward Turner. The Hibbing goalie was not ready for the blow and before he could set himself, Bartholome drove the puck into the meshes." The Minneapolis skater returned to his hometown in 1946 and played four seasons with the Millers before retiring from the professional game. He continued as an amateur for four more seasons.

Earl Bartholome

Edward F. Olson

St. Louis Flyers (1946-1951)
Cleveland Barons (1951-1955)
Victoria Cougars (1955-1956)

Forward

Born: Jan. 1, 1922, Hancock, Mich.

Eddie Olson, one of nine brothers from a great American hockey family, came out of Michigan's Upper Peninsula to create a visibility for Americans in hockey at a time when that visibility was its lowest ebb — the decade of the 1950's. Olson performed principally in the American Hockey League where he attained honors that remain today virtually unmatched for an American player at any level of professional hockey.

While playing for the Cleveland Barons he twice won AHL scoring titles, 1953 and 1955, was AHL MVP, 1953, and was named to the first All-Star Team in both 1953 and 1955. It was no surprise that during these particular years the Barons were Calder Cup champions twice and were in the playoffs during the other year.

The Marquette skater later coached for three seasons, including one with Victoria of the Western Hockey League, making him, at the time, the only known American to coach a professional team in Canada. Olson's brother, Wesley, originated the "kick shot" and the future Hall of Famer used it in his pre-AHL days. He was described by a Vancouver sports writer as the most feared shot in the old Pacific Coast League. The writer said that "Even Ripley wouldn't believe this. Placing his stick firmly on the ice in the shooting position Mr. Olson, rears back like an Army mule, and brings his right foot forward with a crashing intensity on the back of the blade..."

Olson had gotten his start in hockey in his hometown with the Marquette Sentinels. With war breaking out he joined the famed Coast Guard Clippers Team which featured such United States Hockey Hall of Fame enshrinees as Frank Brimsek and John Mariucci. The Clippers played in the Eastern Amateur League and, in 1944, Olson led that circuit with 96 points. The prior season he was team scoring leader with 85 points. After that it was on to the Pacific Coast League and then stardom in the American League, first with St. Louis and then with Cleveland.

Eddie Olson

William J. "Bill" Riley

Dartmouth College (1946-49)

Forward
Referee

Born: October 6, 1921, Medford, Mass.

Bill Riley occupies a unique position as one of the greatest all time scorers in college hockey, as well as one of three famous hockey playing brothers. His brothers, Jack and Joe, were stars at Dartmouth in 1944 and 1949, respectively. Jack went on to coach at West Point, and later piloted the 1960 U.S. Olympic gold medal winners in Squaw Valley. (Jack is also a Hall of Fame enshrinee as well.)

Although a member of the class of 1946, Riley's career at Dartmouth was interrupted by World War II military service. As a result he played during the 1943 season as a freshman and then resumed competition from 1946-49. Playing four varsity seasons, Riley appeared in 71 games, scoring 118 goals and 110 assists for 218 points. He was the team leader in all seasons except 1947. Riley was also a major factor in the Big Green's march to the NCAA finals in both 1948 and 1949 as well. In 1948 Dartmouth met Colorado College in the first round of the first ever NCAA tournament, and emerged 8-4 victors. However in the finals the score was reversed and Michigan took the laurels. The following year the defeat by Michigan was avenged 4-2 in the semifinals, but Eastern rival Boston College won the title 4-3.

During Riley's brilliant college career, Dartmouth compiled a gaudy record of 68-11-2. In that time frame he had scored five goals in a game against Northwestern and Princeton, four versus Boston College, and had ten hat tricks to boot.

Hockey historian S. Kip Farrington even placed him on his all-time Dartmouth team for the period 1945-1970. Following retirement as an active player, the Medford skater continued his interest in the game and later became a leading official in New England Referees' Association. In 1971 he was later named as the commissioner of the New England Amateur League. Riley was previously honored for his contributions to hockey in March 1977 when he received the Sheaffer Pen Award.

THE CLASS OF 1978

Peter Bessone

Pittsburgh Hornets (1937-1942)
Cleveland Barons (1942-46)
Providence Reds (1947-48)

Defenseman

Born: Jan. 13, 1913, New Bradford, Mass.

An all around athlete at West Springfield, Mass., High School in football, baseball and hockey; Peter Bessone went on to a fascinating career in the ice sport at both the international and professional levels. After high school, Bessone played for the West Side Rangers in Springfield before being lured to Europe in 1931. It was in Paris, playing for Stade, France, that the defenseman became the "Babe Ruth" of hockey in Paris. Henri Cochet, the great French tennis player, said of him: "Bessone is an excellent hockey player and is very popular throughout France. He is the biggest drawing card in French hockey."

In February, 1934, he was a late replacement on the United States National Team which finished second to Canada in the World Tournament at Milan, Italy. In the semi-final game against Germany, he scored two goals to pace the 3-0 American win. Bessone returned to the United States in the mid-1930s and played with the amateur Pittsburgh Yellow Jackets, before turning professional with the Iron City's Hornets. He toiled for nine seasons with the Hornets and Cleveland Barons in the American Hockey League, where he gained over 100 penalty minutes in three different seasons.

Following his professional career, Bessone returned to international hockey, coaching teams in France, Switzerland, and Italy. He did return to the United States, however, in 1949, to coach the IHLs Springfield Indians for one season, before hanging em' up for good.

Peter Bessone

Donald M. Clark

Minn. Amateur Hockey Assoc. (1947-1998)
Amateur Hockey Association of the U.S.

Administrator

Born: May 25, 1915, Kensal, N.D.
(Raised: Fairbault, Minn.)

Will Roger's quote "I never met a man I didn't like" is a bit hard for many to accept. And yet it applies so very much to Don Clark. No one in hockey has ever met anyone who didn't like him. Throughout his life he tirelessly traveled the length and breadth of his beloved Minnesota preaching the gospel of amateur hockey. In doing so, he has won countless converts to the game and made a host of friends.

During his boyhood days in Fairbault, Minn., he exhibited an early aptitude for sports, competing in high school football, hockey and baseball. Later, he played amateur baseball in the Southern Minnesota League and amateur hockey in the Twin Cities area. It was in 1947 that he, along with fellow enshrinees Bob Ridder and Everett "Buck" Riley, founded the Minnesota Amateur Hockey Association (MAHA), and proceeded to build it into the most successful organization of its kind in the United States. Among his accomplishments with MAHA, were founding the first Bantam level state tournament in the nation, serving as President from 1954-57 and Secretary-Treasurer from 1949-55 and 1958-74.

An interest in the National aspects of the game also developed in Clark, and in 1958, he was named as the manager of the first U.S. National Team to ever play in the Soviet Union. For nearly three decades he served in many capacities, including vice president, of the Amateur Hockey Association of the United States. His areas of particular interest were in junior and youth hockey. Clark was honored by the National Hockey League in 1975, when he received the Lester Patrick Award for service to hockey in the United States.

Considering the time, interest, and travel that Clark has devoted to hockey, it is not surprising that he has become one of the foremost American hockey historians. As such, much of what is in the United States Hockey Hall of Fame, which he later served as President, came from his impressive collection and knowledge of the records, players, participants, and incidents of the game. It can truthfully be said: "We shall not see another like him."

If John Mariucci is considered to be the "Godfather of Minnesota Hockey," then Don Clark would then have to be the "Grandfather."

Hubert "Hub" Nelson

Minneapolis Millers
Oklahoma City Warriors
St. Louis Flyers
(1930-1942)

Goaltender

Born: August 14, 1907, Minneapolis, Minn.

The figures were simply amazing. Goals against averages of 1.70, 1.80, 2.00, 1.90, etc., etc., etc., posted over a period of 12 years. Here was a man who could stop just about anything shot at him. Of Swedish heritage, Hub was raised in Minneapolis, where he went on to become one of the great American goaltenders.

"Hub" first donned the pads at age 12 in Park Board play. After that, it was on to high school where the future Hall of Famer was to play on two championship teams and be named to the All City Team on two occasions. Turning professional with the Minneapolis Millers of the Central League in 1930, Nelson went on to play 12 brilliant seasons in both the Central League and American Hockey Association. Over that period of time, he recorded a lifetime regular season average of 1.87, while blanking the opposition in nearly 25% of all games played.

In 1939, with the St. Louis Flyers, Nelson blanked opposing teams an amazing 18 times in 48 regular-season games. The previous year, he had done almost as well with 15 shutouts in the same number of games. Needless to say, such heroics gained Nelson All-Star honors on eight different occasions. During World War II, he served with Hall of Famers John Mariucci, Eddie Olson, and Frank Brimsek on the famed Coast Guard Cutters team.

With such a brilliant career, the question is asked: "Why didn't he play in the NHL?" The answer: Both the New York Rangers and Chicago Blackhawks made repeated attempts to buy Nelson while he was with St. Louis, but the management there chose to keep him rather than give him his opportunity in the majors. One can understand this reluctance when reading this excerpt from a St. Louis newspaper: "Nelson, the goalie, has not an equal in the league in the last 10 years. He enjoyed his greatest season and perhaps was more responsible than any other member of the team for keeping the Flyers ahead of the procession from the start of the campaign."

Nelson retired after his Coast Guard career and devoted his time to business interests in Minneapolis.

THE CLASS OF 1979

Robert E. "Bob" Dill

Springfield (AHL) (1941-42), Buffalo (AHL) (1942-44), New York Rangers (NHL) (1944-45), St. Paul (USHL) (1946-50)

Defenseman

Born: April 25, 1920, St. Paul, Minn.

Bob Dill is one of those relatively rare athletes who successfully combined a two sport professional career in both hockey and baseball. After graduating from St. Paul's Cretin High School, Dill went on to play the ice sport in Florida's little known Tropical Ice Hockey League and then moved into the Eastern Amateur League with Baltimore, where he remained for his nine years. Dill then turned pro with Springfield, of the American Hockey League, and played there and at Buffalo for three more years.

(On the baseball side of things Dill played the outfield for both Minneapolis and Indianapolis in the American Association and later served as a minor league manager.)

In January of 1944, the New York Rangers gave up four players to Buffalo to get the fighting Irishman, and he played there through the end of the 1945 season. A nephew of Mike Gibbons, a former Minnesota boxing legend, Dill, too, was a notorious brawler. Returning to his native Minnesota, Dill played five outstanding seasons with the St. Paul Saints of the United States Hockey League. In both 1947 and 1950 he was a first team all-star, while in 1949 he anchored the defense as the Saints won the league playoff championship. Always an offensive-minded defenseman, Dill enjoyed his finest goal scoring season in 1949, when he scored 15 goals.

Retiring after the 1950 season, Dill went on to later work with the NHL's Minnesota North Stars as a scout.

Bobby Dill

John P. "Jack" Riley, Jr.

Dartmouth College (1940-1944)
U.S. Military Academy (1950-86)
U.S. Olympic Team (1960)

Coach

Born: June 15, 1920, Boston, Mass.

Jack Riley was an outstanding college player at Dartmouth from 1940-44. The Boston native went on to compete on the 1948 Olympic Team, which finished fourth at St. Moritz, Switzerland, and then served as the player-coach of the 1949 National Team which gained a third place finish at the World Tournament at Stockholm, Sweden.

From there Riley went on to join the staff of the U.S. Military Academy in 1950, where he became head coach in 1951, and remained until 1986, when he passed the reigns to his son Rob. Over that span at Army, he was twice named as the NCAA Coach of the Year. Incredibly, he posted just six losing seasons in his 36 years at West Point, and at the time of his retirement, his 541 career wins were second only to Michigan Tech's John McInnes in the history of NCAA hockey.

Perhaps the highlight of his storied career, however, came at Squaw Valley, in 1960, when he led an underdog American team past the likes of several of the world's great ice powers — Canada, Russia, Czechoslovakia and Sweden, to capture the country's first gold medal in Olympic hockey competition.

From the preliminary Olympic training camps 22 players were selected to attend the final camp at West Point, New York. Under Riley's tutelage the squad was pared to 17 members by early January before departing on an 18-game exhibition tour. Riley's squad swept undefeated through the preliminary and championship rounds to the gold medal victory. The pivotal game in the series was the clash against Russia. With 10,000 fans jamming Blyth Arena and a national television audience on hand the game proved to be a classic. Coach Riley best describes the final minutes:

"The 5' 10," 145 lb. Billy Christian foiled goalie Puchkov again at 14:59 of the last period. Getting the puck on a play set up by his brother Roger and by Williams (Tom), Billy outsmarted Puchkov again when the goalie came out to cut down the angle of the shot. The puck went in, and our players and the jubilant crowd jumped for joy. That was it, as McCartan and the stalwart defensemen fought off the Russians the rest of the way." Then, a come from behind 9-4 victory over the Czechs that next day proved to be the clincher.

THE CLASS OF 1980

Walter L. Bush, Jr.

Manager, U.S. National/Olympic Teams (1959-1964)
President, Minnesota North Stars (1967-83)
AHAUS & USA Hockey (1960-Present)

Administrator

Born: September 25, 1929, Minneapolis, Minn.

Known widely as the primary founder of the Minnesota North Stars, Walter Bush found success in hockey as a prep school player, college and amateur player, amateur coach and Olympic manager, before getting into the executive side of the sport. The Minneapolis native began his hockey career at the Breck School and continued at Dartmouth. While working on his law degree at the University of Minnesota, he kept his skates sharp by playing senior hockey and helping to organize the U.S. Central League. He then became active on the international scene, managing the 1959 U.S. National Team and the 1964 U.S. Olympic Team, serving on the U.S. Olympic Committee in 1963, and later a four year term on the USOC's Hockey section. He has also participated as president and vice president of the Minnesota Amateur Hockey Association and as a director of the Amateur Hockey Association of the United States.

Instrumental in bringing professional hockey to Minnesota in the form of the Minneapolis Bruins, Bush later put all his credentials to work in securing an NHL franchise for Minnesota in 1967, the North Stars.

Among his many awards and accolades, Bush was the first "grass roots American" to win the Lester Patrick Trophy, which he received in 1973; was named as the NHL's Executive of the Year in 1972 by the Hockey News; and was enshrined into the Hockey Hall of Fame in Toronto in the year 2000. In addition, Bush has also served as the President of USA Hockey for the better part of the 1990s. A man with a true passion, he is a real Minnesota hockey legend.

Walter Bush

Frank W. "Nick" Kahler

Duluth Curling Club (1913-1914)
St. Paul Athletic Club (1914-1920)
Minneapolis Millers (1920-1927 & 1936-37)
Augsburg College (1927-1928)

Administrator

Born: March 14, 1891, Dollar Bay, Mich.

Hailing from Michigan's Copper Country, Nick Kahler was a high scoring center for every team he played on. He achieved "star" status at a very early age, was very popular with both the press and the fans, and invariably was elected captain by his teammates on nearly every team he played on.

Kahler was a promoter, often recruiting to build a team and fan attention. While he played with greats like fellow enshrinees: Joe Linder, "Moose" Goheen, Tony Conroy, and Vic Des Jardins, he also encouraged, coached, and managed such greats as "Ching" Johnson, Lyle Wright, "Taffy" Abel, Virgil Johnson, Phil Perkins, and Andy Mulligan.

Kahler's earliest years were spent playing amateur hockey in the Copper Country and in Canada before joining the Duluth Curling Club for the 1914 season. From there it was on to St. Paul to play with the Athletic Club as manager, coach, and player. In 1916 the Athletic Club, with Moose Goheen, Tony Conroy, Eddie Fitzgerald, and Kahler won the coveted McNaughton Cup against Sault Ste. Marie, Michigan, and then went on to defeat Lachine, Quebec, for the Art Ross Trophy. He continued with the Athletic Club until 1920 and was selected for the 1920 Olympic Team, but financial obligations precluded his participation.

In 1920 Kahler launched the Minneapolis Millers in the United States Amateur Hockey Association. His 1925 team won the league title, but the start of professional hockey in the United States brought a quick end to the Millers by the end of the 1927 season. Kahler was selected to coach the Augsburg College team to represent the United States in the 1928 Olympics, but the decision was ultimately made to send no team. Kahler returned to hockey for one year in the late 1930's as owner of the now professional Millers, and saw his team capture the American Hockey Association title.

In addition to his hockey interests, Kahler founded Golden Gloves boxing in Minnesota as well as the Northwest Sports Show in Minneapolis. He was inducted into the Minnesota Sports Hall of Fame in 1962 and awarded the Governor's Public Service Citation and Heritage Award in 1967.

THE CLASS OF 1981

Robert "Bob" Cleary

Harvard University (1955-1958)
United States National Olympic Teams (1959-1960)

Forward

Born: April 21, 1936, Cambridge, Mass.

Bob Cleary was one of the great college players to come out of the East in the post-World War II era. Playing three varsity seasons at Belmont Hill prep school, he led his team to three consecutive Massachusetts private school titles. At the same time he played on the National AHAUS Junior Champion Cusick team from 1952-54. From there it was on to Harvard and three memorable seasons under coach Ralph "Cooney" Weiland. Over the course of his career at Harvard Cleary scored 202 points on 100 goals and 102 assists. In both 1957 and 1958, his point totals were enough to lead the nation in scoring. The team captain was named to the prestigious All-American team at center as well in 1958.

In both the previously cited seasons Cleary's ability and leadership brought the Crimson to the NCAA tournament where they placed fourth both years. During his college career Cleary was also named All-East in 1957 and 1958, as well as receiving the prestigious Walter Brown Trophy in both seasons. That award, named after an enshrinee of the Hall of Fame, is given to the outstanding American player at an Eastern college.

Cleary was also a key member of the 1959 United States National Team which finished fourth in the World Tournament at Prague. A late addition to the 1960 Olympic Team, Cleary teamed with his brother Bill and former Harvard linemate Bob McVey to form one of the upstart Americans most effective lines. Cleary finished third in scoring during the Olympic tournament with five goals and three assists. His brother, Bill, was also inducted into the Hall of Fame, just five years earlier.

Bob Cleary

William M. Jennings

President: New York Rangers (1962-1981)
Chairman: NHL Board of Gov's (1968-70)

Administrator

Born: December 14, 1920, New York, NY.

As one of the most influential and active governors in the National Hockey League, Bill Jennings emerged as the architect of the league's dramatic expansion during the late 1960s into the late 1970s. He served as chairman of the league's Board of Governors from 1968-1970, in addition to serving on or chairing virtually every other league committee during that same era. In 1966, Jennings originated the NHL's Lester Patrick Award Dinner, which annually honors persons for "outstanding service to hockey in the United States." He won the Lester Patrick Award himself in 1971.

He was also instrumental in the establishment of the New York office of the NHL in 1964 and in the establishment of the Metropolitan Junior Hockey Association, as well as in the continued development of amateur hockey in the Metropolitan New York area. Besides his distinguished hockey career, Jennings was active for over 25 years in the conduct of professional golf tournaments for the benefit of Westchester County hospitals. In 1967, he founded the Westchester Golf Classic and served as its general chairman, raising nearly $4,000,000 for the participating Golfers' Association of America.

In addition to his sporting interests, the Princeton graduate was a senior partner of the New York City law firm of Simpson Thacher & Bartlett, and a director of various major corporations. He was also honorary chairman of United Hospital in Port Chester, N.Y. His contemporaries said it best of Bill Jennings: "He is one of professional hockey's most dynamic and successful executives for more than two decades, and has proven a most influential force in the dramatic and successful operation and expansion of professional hockey, in general, and the National Hockey League in particular."

The National Hockey League previously recognized Jennings' contribution by naming him to the Hockey Hall of Fame in Toronto in 1976.

Thomas M. Williams

Boston Bruins, Minnesota North Stars, California Golden Seals, Washington Capitals, New England Whalers: (1962-76)

Forward

Born: April 17, 1940, Duluth, Minn.

When Tommy Williams broke into the Boston Bruins lineup during the 1962 season, he became the first American to play regularly in the National Hockey League since his fellow enshrinee, Frank Brimsek, retired from the Chicago Black Hawks in April, of 1950. When his NHL career ended with the Washington Capitals in 1976, he stood at the top of the list of NHL American developed players in goals and points scored, with 115 goals and 253 points, respectively. The Duluth native was developed as a player by his father, Warren "Rip" Williams, who literally made the old cliché "I taught him everything he knew," a living reality.

While starting in high school hockey at Duluth Central, the highly talented skater soon was playing in senior competition with men years his senior. He was a natural selection for the 1960 United States Olympic Team, when, as an 18-year-old, he played on a line with the fabled Christian brothers (also both enshrinees) of Warroad, Minn. Williams assisted on Bill Christian's goal which defeated the Russians, 3-2, as the U.S. went on to win its first gold medal.

Originally intending to play college hockey at the University of Minnesota, the young Olympian was persuaded to try pro hockey. After a year and a half at Kingston, Ontario, of the old Eastern Pro League, he was called up to the parent Bruins.

"I can recall my first game with the Bruins," said Williams. "We beat Chicago, 5-4, in Boston, and I scored two goals. I didn't sleep all night. Another highlight for me was once in the playoffs against Montreal when I was named the first star."

There were many more outstanding games for the versatile forward, who played all three up front positions, in his 16-year professional career. Williams saw service with Boston, Minnesota, California, and Washington in the NHL.

"I played before expansion," he said on his retirement. "I played hockey because I was good at it, and I was fortunate to do something for a long number of years that I enjoyed. How many guys can say they enjoyed a job for 16 years?" Williams remains as one of Minnesota's greatest all-time players.

THE CLASS OF 1982

Calvin C. Marvin

Coach, Manager-Warroad Lakers (1946-98)
Coach, United States National Team (1958)
Manager, United States National Team (1965)
Administrator
Born: April 29, 1924, Warroad, Minn.

Cal Marvin has become synonymous with the Warroad Lakers, the most successful senior amateur hockey team in U.S. history. After returning from World War II service with the Marine Corps, Marvin helped found the team and later served as sometimes coach and all times general manager for more than 50 years. The team never had a losing season and reached the heights of amateur achievement on several occasions by winning the 1955 United States Intermediate title; the Canadian Intermediate Championships in both 1964 and 1974, and the Allen Cup three times in a row from 1994-96.

The Lakers, who provided countless Minnesota kids the opportunity to play at the highest possible amateur level, featured many future and former NHL and Olympic players on its roster through the years. In addition, nearly every Olympic and National team over the past 40 years made the trek to the tiny northwestern Minnesota town to play the fabled club.

A couple of the most famous Laker alumni were the Christian brothers: Billy and Roger, both of whom are also enshrined in the Hall as well. Others include David Christian (Bill's son), and Henry Boucha, both NHL veterans.

It has been said that Cal would do absolutely anything for the cause of hockey. Marvin's unique talents have not gone unnoticed on the national level. He coached the 1958 United States National Team (the first American athletic team to play in the Soviet Union), to a fifth place finish in the World Tournament, and in 1965 was selected as manager of that year's national team.

A true legend, he will forever be known as the Godfather of Warroad hockey.

Cal Marvin

William J. Stewart

Coach, Chicago Blackhawks (1937-39)
Coach, United States National Team (1957)
Referee, NHL (1928-1937, 1939-1941)

Coach, Referee

Born: Sept. 26, 1894, Fitchburg, Mass.

For 22 days in late March and early April, of 1938, Coach Bill Stewart was the leader of a largely unknown and little regarded group of Chicago Blackhawks hockey players that brought an unexpected Stanley Cup to the Windy City. In doing so he became the first American-developed coach in the history of the National Hockey League to capture hockey's top prize. Stewart's underdog Blackhawks upset the Montreal Canadians two game to one, the New York Americans two games to one, and the Toronto Maple Leafs three games to one on the trail to the Stanley Cup. The Blackhawks had barely qualified for the play-offs winning only 14 games, losing 25, and tying nine. Despite that, they finished ahead of the Detroit Red Wings in the American Division of the league and qualified for the Stanley Cup playoffs.

Bill Stewart

Among Chicago's lineup were four players who would later be enshrined in the United States Hockey Hall of Fame: goalie Mike Karakas (Eveleth, MN), forwards Carl "Cully" Dahlstrom (Minneapolis) and Elwin "Doc" Romnes (White Bear Lake, MN), and defenseman Virgil Johnson (Minneapolis). In addition, Vic Heyliger (Concord, Mass.) also saw service of a team that became the first American oriented team to ever win Lord Stanley's Cup.

Stewart had began his hockey career in 1921 officiating hockey games in the Boston area. His proficiency was such that by 1928 he was appointed a referee in the National Hockey League. He would hold that position until 1941 with time out for his stint as Chicago's coach. The Fitchburg native had prior coaching experience at Milton Academy and throughout Massachusetts hockey.

Later, in 1957, Stewart led the United States National Team to a 23-3-1 record, but the team was prevented by the State Department from participating in the World Tournament because of the Soviet intervention in Hungary.

Bill Stewart was also well known as a baseball umpire serving in the National League from 1933 to 1954. During this period he even umpired the 1933. 1937, 1948, and 1953 World Series. But to hockey people he will always be remembered as the man who blazed the trail for today's NHL American Coaches — fellow enshrinees Herb Brooks and Bob Johnson among them.

THE CLASS OF 1983

Oscar J. Almquist

Roseau, (Minn.) High School (1941-1967)

Coach

Born: March 7, 1908, Eveleth, Minn.

Oscar Almquist grew up playing hockey in Eveleth (Minn.), and went on to star as a goalie for the high school team from 1923-27. After a two-year interval with Virginia of the Arrowhead Amateur League, he entered St. Mary's College in Winona, Minn. At St. Mary's, he played four varsity years and was named both team captain and to the All American team in 1933.

Almquist returned to Northeastern Minnesota after graduation to begin a four-year professional career, first with hometown Eveleth Rangers in the Central League, followed by three seasons with the St. Paul Saints in the American Hockey Association. During this period he was named to league all star teams in both the 1934 and 1936 seasons. The coaching career, for which he would become legendary, began at Williams, Minn., in 1937, followed by Roseau, in 1938, where he coached the high school "B" team until 1941, while at the same time playing for the amateur Cloverleafs. In 1941, the Eveleth native became Roseau's head coach, a position he would hold until 1967. During this period Roseau High School became a perennial power winning state titles in 1946, 1958, 1959, and 1961. Roseau appeared in the state event fourteen times, and in addition to the state championships they were runner-ups on four occasions, third place finishers once, and captured two consolation titles.

When Almquist gave up coaching to become strictly athletic director and high school principal, his teams had posted a record of 404 wins, 148 losses, and 21 ties., including a 49-game winning streak from 1957-59. A member of the Minnesota Hockey Coaches Hall of Fame, the "Big-O" was truly a "Giant of the North."

Oscar Almquist

John W. "Jack" McCartan

United States Olympic Team (1960)
New York Rangers (1960-1961)
Minnesota Fighting Saints (1972-1974)
Various minor professional teams (1962-72)

Goaltender

Born: August 5, 1935, St. Paul, Minn.

In February of 1960, University of Minnesota goaltender Jack McCartan was the driving force behind a group of unknown and unheralded hockey players who represented the United States at the Squaw Valley Olympics. As a college player for the Golden Gophers, he had twice been named to the All American team, but nonetheless was a late addition to the 1960 Olympic team. Playing before partisan crowds, the underdog United States team upset Canada, the Soviet Union, and Czechoslovakia to capture America's first gold medal in hockey. The first indications that this was to be a different hockey Olympics came against Canada.

The United States had defeated the "hockey motherland" in the 1956 Olympics and the Canadians were keying for the rematch. McCartan made 39 stops, many of them of the unbelievable category, as the U.S. won, 2-1, and built momentum toward the gold medal. In the nationally televised game against the Soviets, he made 27 saves, as in the words of the UPI reporter covering the game: "Late in the period, McCartan had to fight like a cornered lion as the Russians drove in savagely on the attack. It was a furious interval, but big Jack stood up —and laid down — under their bristling fire to hold them off."

Jack Riley, the gold medal coach, said of McCartan: "He was the most outstanding goalie I've ever seen. Without him we wouldn't have been successful at Squaw Valley."

After the Olympics McCartan embarked on a 15-year career in professional hockey. Appearing briefly in two different seasons with the New York Rangers, he was sent to Kitchener-Waterloo of the Eastern Professional League. In 1961, he had a sparkling 2.78 average in 52 games. The following season he led the league in shutouts with five. Over the next decade, the St. Paul native played primarily in the Western League, also appearing in the Central League and World Hockey Association. In 1969 he garnered second team Western League goaltending honors, while in both 1970 and 1971 he captured first team honors, all with San Diego. He concluded his professional career in 1974 with the Minnesota Fighting Saints of the World Hockey Association.

THE CLASS OF 1984

William D. "Billy" Christian

U.S. National/Olympic Teams (1958-1965)
Warroad Lakers (1956-1980)
Forward
Born: January 29, 1938, Warroad, Minn.

Mention the name Christian to American hockey followers and there is instantaneous recognition. After leading his Warroad high school team to the state tournament finals in 1953, Billy Christian played one year at the University of Minnesota under Coach John Mariucci before joining the 1958 United States National Team — the first American team to ever play in the Soviet Union.

Bill was the team's leading scorer with seven goals and five assists, as the squad finished with a respectable 3-3-1 record in the World Tournament at Oslo, Norway. That would mark the first of five National/Olympic teams on which Christian participated, with the others coming in 1960, 1962, 1964 and 1965. But, it is, of course, 1960 that is best remembered, as Billy helped to guide the fabled squad to the gold medal by scoring the tying and game-winning goals against the Russians — the latter coming on an assist from his brother, Roger.

Christian later played for his hometown Warroad Lakers for 23 years before finally retiring after the 1980 season. The team never had a losing season during this period and won Canadian Intermediate title in both 1964 and 1974. In both 1969 and 1970, Bill was the All Star coach as the Lakers were Manitoba Senior Hockey League champions. With the Lakers he had the good fortune to play with both his sons, Eddie and David. Both sons played college hockey with David going on to a professional career in the NHL.

In 1964, with other family members, he helped found Christian Brothers, Inc., today a multi-million dollar hockey stick and equipment manufacturing company. He continues his work for hockey through community service, and also through youth coaching — which he has done on and off at youth levels for several decades in Warroad.

Billy Christian

William W. Wirtz

Chicago Blackhawks (1967-92)

Administrator

Born: October 5, 1929, Chicago, Ill.

When the Wirtz family purchased the Chicago Blackhawks in 1954, they became a part of the team with a unique American heritage in professional hockey. The 1938 edition of the club won the Stanley Cup and produced six members of the United States Hockey Hall of Fame: Mike Karakas, Cully Dahlstom, Doc Romnes, Virgil Johnson, Vic Heyliger, and Coach Bill Stewart.

Bill Wirtz

Bill assumed that proud tradition when he became team president in 1967, taking over this active role from his father Arthur, who went on to become Chairman of the Board. He had taken an active part in hockey and the Blackhawks since his graduation from Brown University in 1950. As president, Bill found himself more and more involved in the daily operations of the game. But Bill's interest in the game goes far beyond the natural concerns for his own team. As Chairman of the National Hockey League Board of Governors, he spent many long hours dealing with hockey problems on the league level. As Chairman, he dealt with such matters as player negotiations, expansion and the myriad of problems that developed on the international hockey front.

His fellow owners elected him to nine terms as Chairman over an 18-year period. He also worked tirelessly on the operation of their home ice at Chicago Stadium — improving the facility over his tenure with such additions as air conditioning, new seating, comfort facilities and expanded parking.

Bill later served as a member of the 1980 and 1984 United States Olympic Ice Hockey Committees. He was also very proud when the Blackhawks signed Ed Olczyk, a 1984 Olympic team member and Chicago native, to a professional contract — making him their first selection in the 1984 entry draft.

Along with his father and brother, Michael, Bill was also very active in harness racing both as a breeder and in the racing end of the sport. One of their greatest breeding accomplishments was the development of Governor Skipper, which was named pacer of the year in 1977.

Wirtz was elected to the Hockey Hall of Fame as a builder in 1976 and was awarded the Lester Patrick Trophy for contributions to hockey in the U.S. in 1978. (Both honors were also bestowed to his father as well.)

THE CLASS OF 1985

Louis Robert "Bob" Blake

Hibbing, Boston, Minneapolis (1933-1943)
Cleveland, Buffalo, Houston, Cincinnati, Pittsburgh (1945-1951)

Forward

Born: August 16, 1916, Ashland, Wis. (Raised in Hibbing, Minn.)

After starring as a three-sport star at Hibbing (Minn.) High School, Bob Blake's professional career began in 1933 at the age of 17 when he joined the hometown Miners of the Central Hockey League. After moving into the top 10 in league scoring, Boston Bruins scout Perk Galbraith signed him to a contract with the Bruins farm club, the Boston Cubs, where Blake led the team to a pair of league titles in as many seasons before joining the Minneapolis Millers in 1937.

    The Cleveland Barons bought the speedy winger's contract during the 1938 season, and he responded by leading the club to the International-American League title in 1939.

    The 1941 season began what was to become a long love affair between Blake and the city of Buffalo. That's when he came to the American A League Bisons after the start of the season. Injuries depleted the defensive corps and he was switched to defense with great success. Blake's speed, durability, and aggressive play made him a great fan favorite. He was selected Buffalo's most popular player in 1942 and captained the team that season and the following when they won the championship.

    After two years off for World War II service in the Pacific with the Army Air Corps, Blake rejoined Buffalo for another championship year late in the 1946 season. Blake was a Bison star for two more seasons before moving to Houston for the 1948 season. His steady play that year helped the team win the United States Hockey League's Loudan Trophy. Many critics rated him the best defenseman in the league.

Bob Blake

Richard "Dick" Rondeau

Dartmouth College (1940-44)
San Diego Seahawks (1944-45)

Born: December 18, 1921, Providence, RI.

If it were not for Eddie Jeremiah, another United States Hockey Hall of Fame enshrinee and long-time Dartmouth Coach, Dick Rondeau might have wound up starring for the Boston Bruins rather than becoming one of Dartmouth's all time greats. Rondeau had come out of Mt. St. Charles Academy in Woonsocket, Rhode Island as a heralded high school player. In 1939, his senior year, he centered the second line and was named All-State center on a team composed entirely of Mr. St. Charles players. Mt. St. Charles was proclaimed unofficial nation champions based on their record of 21 wins and two losses as Rondeau won the league scoring title with 27 goals and 11 assists.

The following year Rondeau was ineligible for further high school competition and joined the Boston Junior Olympics, then a Bruins' farm team. The Olympics played the major Eastern colleges and were runners-up in the national junior tournament. It was then that Eddie Jeremiah entered the picture convincing Rondeau to enroll at Dartmouth, rather than continuing with the Olympics. After a solid freshmen season, the winger centered the famous line of Jack Riley, also a United States Hockey Hall of Fame member, and Bill Harrison, as Dartmouth was proclaimed national champions in 1942. The team won 21 games and lost two while Rondeau led the nation in scoring with 45 goals and 32 assists. But there was more to come as Dartmouth was on a roll which would see them win 41 consecutive games over a four year period.

Rondeau captained the 1943 team as well, and also served as coach when Jeremiah entered the Navy in mid-season. (He was captain again in 1944.) Over his four-year college career Rondeau shattered nearly all of the school's scoring records, tallying 103 goals and 73 assists for an average 4.4 points per game.

After graduation Rondeau entered the Marine Corps and played for San Diego in the Pacific Coast League while stationed in California. A recreational swimming accident ended his active playing career in 1945, but not his involvement with the sport. The post war year saw him involved as a coach at both Holy Cross and Providence College and as a linesman in the American Hockey League. He later moved to Texas, where he continued to remain active in youth hockey and as a minor official in the Central League.

Harold "Hal" Trumble

Administrator

Born: August 28, 1926, Minneapolis, Minn.

When Hal Trumble took over the reigns of the Amateur Hockey Association of the United States (AHAUS), it was largely a part-time operation operating deep into the red. Thanks to Trumble, however, he turned the association into a prosperous full-time, professionally staffed organization headquartered in its own building in Colorado Springs, Colorado. The dramatic turnaround was a direct result of Trumble's driving, professional competence, as he went on to become the organization's first full-time executive director.

AHAUS would become the national governing body for hockey as the game's exclusive member to the U.S. Olympic Committee (USOC) and the International Ice Hockey Federation (IIHF). Under Trumble's direction, AHAUS grew from 7,015 teams in 1972 to 11,543 in 1985. During that same time span, referee registration has increased from 3,178 to 8,434 and a complete program of coaching and referee clinics as well as hockey publications were also developed.

On the international level, the United States won the Olympic gold medal in 1980 and has iced strong teams in the ensuing Olympiads as well as in World Tournaments.

Trumble enjoyed hockey at an early age and played through high school and senior amateur hockey in the 1950's. When his playing days were over he began officiating, first in high school, then at the college level, and finally internationally. His officiating career included refereeing both the gold and bronze medal games in the 1968 Olympics. Such experience led him to service as Technical Director of the International Ice Hockey Federation Referees' Committee from 1972-82.

In addition to his officiating expertise, Trumble was active at the team management level. He managed the 1972 U.S. Olympic Team which won the silver medal at Sapporo, Japan. That team featured such future NHL regulars as Henry Boucha, Robbie Ftorek, and Mark Howe. In 1983 Trumble returned to team management as the United States won the "B" Pool tournament and the right to advance to the "A" Pool for the 1984 Olympics.

A man of many interests, Trumble was also an international caliber baseball and softball umpire. In addition, he served as President of the National Council of the Youth Sports Directors in 1981.

THE CLASS OF 1986

John P. "Jack" Garrity

United States Olympic Team (1948)
Boston University (1949-1952)
Senior Amateur Teams (1952-1965)

Forward

Born: April 1, 1926, Woburn, Mass.

Jack Garrity was an outstanding high school player who moved on to play both international and college hockey at the highest level. After leading Medford, (Mass.) High School to a pair of state championships in 1943 and 1944, Garrity continued in Senior hockey after W.W.II service. Coming off the roster of the Needham, (Mass.) Rockets, he was just one of three non-college players to make the 1948 United States Olympic Team, which narrowly missed the Bronze medal finishing with a 5-3 record.

Garrity then enrolled at Boston University in 1949 and was quickly named Freshman Team captain. The following year he broke the then-existing NCAA single-season scoring record with 51 goals and 33 assists as BU went all the way to the NCAA Finals before bowing to Colorado College. In 1952 the co-captain led BU to another Final Four, but the team lost out in the semi-finals to Michigan. Garrity was named an All American and All NCAA Tournament Team selection in both 1951 and 1952.

Garrity graduated in 1952 and played the following year with the senior Boston Olympics. Over the next 13 years he played senior amateur hockey with various teams, most notably Brockton and Rockland, who both won National Senior AHAUS titles in 1959 and 1960 respectively. During that period he began another hockey career as an official on the amateur, high school, and college levels. He also got into coaching at the high school and senior amateur levels as well.

Jack Garrity

Kenneth J. Yackel

University of Minnesota (1950-1955)
United States Olympic Team (1952)
Minor pro teams (1955-60)
Boston Bruins (1958-59)
Minneapolis Millers (1960-63)

Forward-Defenseman

Born: March 5, 1932, St. Paul, Minn.

Kenny Yackel

Ken Yackel graduated as a three-sport star from Humboldt High School (St. Paul) in 1949 and went on to greatness at the University of Minnesota as both a defenseman and forward on the Gopher hockey team. Minnesota, who was coached by fellow enshrinee John Mariucci, reached the final four of the NCAA Tournament in both 1953 and 1954 with Yackel playing a major role. He was named to the All Tournament Team in 1954 while at the same time being selected to the All American Team.

Yackel was just one of two American-developed players to appear in the NHL in the decade of the 1950's, when he played with Boston in 1959. His other professional play included service with Cleveland and Providence in the American League as well as Saskatoon/St. Paul of the Western League.

In the early 1960's Yackel coached and played in the (technically) amateur International League for the Minneapolis Millers. In 1961 the Millers won the regular season championship, as Yackel garnered the league scoring title and first all-star team honors as the team's player/coach. The following year he had a career high 50 goals and was named to the league all-star team at left wing.

In 1963 Yackel coached the Millers to the finals before losing to Fort Wayne, but his 100 point season was sufficient to gain second team all star honors at both left wing and coach.

Also active on the international scene, Yackel was a member of the 1952 United States Olympic Team that won a silver medal, losing only to Czechoslovakia and tying Canada. In 1965, he coached the United States National Team in the world tournament at Tampere, Finland.

Then, late in 1971, he answered the call of his alma mater and filled in as interim coach for the balance of Minnesota's season. He remained active in the hockey community not only in his native Minnesota, but also nationally. He also devoted a lot of his hockey interests to the advancement of the John Mariucci Inner City Hockey Assoc., a program designed to encourage hockey development among inner-city youth. He is one of Minnesota's greatest all-around athletes.

THE CLASS OF 1987

John "Jack" Kirrane, Jr.

United States Olympic Team (1948, 1960)
United States National Team (1957, 1963)
Various Senior Teams

Defenseman

Born: August 20, 1928, Brookline, Mass.

Jack Kirrane practically grew up on skates. His father, the late John J. Kirrane, Sr., a captain in the Brookline, Mass., Fire Department, was an ardent hockey enthusiast who annually flooded the backyard of the family's Clyde Street residence. The elder Kirrane was also the expert who made sure the ice was right and the hockey sticks shellacked to make them last longer. It was in such a tradition that Jack and his brothers learned the game.

Jack progressed on to Brookline High School where he earned All Scholastic and Most Valuable Player honors in the Eastern Schoolboy Hockey League. After high school it was on to the Boston Junior Olympics and a subsequent spot on the 1948 Olympic Team. Only 17 at the time, Kirrane was a teammate of United States Hockey Hall of Fame enshrinees Jack Garrity, Jack Riley, and Manager Walter Brown, as the team finished fourth with a 5-3 record.

However, it was to be the 1960 Olympics for which Jack Kirrane would be remembered. An underdog United States team stunned the hockey world by upsetting Canada and the Soviet Union to bring America its then greatest hockey success since the 1933 World Tournament victory. In the 3-2 win over the Soviets it was said of Jack Kirrane that regardless of personal safety, he threw his body into the path of Russian shots time after time in order to take the heat off goalie Jack McCartan. His defensive partner, John Mayasich, commented: "He was a team player and catalyst of the '60 Olympic team. He was one of the older players on that team and he was all serious. Defensively he was one of the best."

Kirrane also played on the 1957 and 1963 National Teams and continued his local hockey career with such Massachusetts senior teams as the Wetzell Club of Brockton, Lynn, Estes, and Lowell. He also led the Wetzells to the 1957 Amateur Hockey Association of the United States National Senior Championship.

Jack Kirrane

Hugh "Muzz" Murray

Sault Ste. Marie (1912-13)
Seattle Metropolitans (1918-21)
Calgary Tigers (1921-22)
Tulsa Oilers (1932-33)

Defenseman-Forward

Born: October 1, 1892, Michigan

The Upper Peninsula of Michigan was an early spawning ground for hockey in the United States. The first professional hockey league in the world, the International League, was even centered there under the guidance of United States Hockey Hall of Fame enshrinee Dr. J.L. (Doc) Gibson. It was under such influence that American greats such as Joe Linder, Nick Kahler, Taffy Abel, and "Muzz" Murray were developed.

"Muzz" Murray was only the second American developed player to participate in the Stanley Cup Finals when he played for the Seattle Metropolitans in the historic 1919 series against the Montreal Canadians. (The series was suspended at 2-2-1 due to an influenza epidemic.) Murray was the third leading scorer in the series and subsequently appeared in the 1920 Finals against Ottawa. After one more season with Seattle, he closed his professional career with Calgary of the Western Canada League in 1922.

He later played briefly for Tulsa in the American Hockey Association. It was Murray's brilliant play as a cover point (defenseman) with Sault Ste. Marie, Mich., of the American Amateur Hockey Association, however, that brought him to pro hockey in the Pacific Coast League. Between 1912-1918, playing in the Western Division of the Association, then the highest level of competition in the United States, Murray was a consistent standout.

An early press account said of him: "Muzz" Murray with his energetic outburst of speed and his remarkable elusive power starred for the Soo. "Muzz" proved the effectiveness of his rushes by scoring one of the Soo's goals after bringing the puck the entire length of the rink and passing all the Calumet players." Murray captained the 1915 Soo team to the Western Division championship before losing to Cleveland in the finals. He was also named to the All-Western team of the American Hockey Association for that season.

The Michigan native was known as both a rough and tumble player as well as a scorer. His spirit, fire and drive made him a team leader. Another early writer noted this when he said: "Muzz" Murray took an ugly slide into the boards striking his face on the side. His nose was injured and also his head. Another time he got a jab in the mouth with a stick, but none of these retarded his playing in the least."

Murray continued playing local senior amateur hockey until he was nearly 60-years-old, while serving the city of Sault Ste. Marie as Superintendent of Streets. He also took an active role in the development of youth hockey in his hometown as well.

Muzz Murray

THE CLASS OF 1988

Richard J. Desmond

Dartmouth College (1945-1950)
United States National Team (1950)
United States Olympic Team (1952)

Goaltender

Born: March 2, 1927, Medford, Mass.

After starring as an all-state goaltender at Medford High School, Richard Desmond, who was also named as the state's most valuable player, went on to play at Vermont Academy in Saxton River in 1945. From there he went on to play at Dartmouth College, when the Big Green was a hockey power in the East.

He was instrumental in Dartmouth's success from 1945-50, and even led the school to a share of the North American Hockey title with the University of Toronto in 1947. He then led Dartmouth to the NCAA Finals in 1949, where he was selected as an All-Ivy League goaltender.

Desmond was also active on the International scene as a member of the 1950 National team which won the silver medal in the World Hockey Tournament in London. There, he served as the team's only goalie, and, after letting in just 12 goals in seven games, was named as the tourney's most valuable player.

Desmond was then placed on temporary duty from the Air Force with the 1952 United States Olympic team, which won the silver medal in Oslo, losing only to Czechoslovakia and tying Canada. All in all, in his 60 games with the squad, he had an impressive 2.98 goal against average.

Dick and his family later made their residence in Palo Verdes, California, where he continued to give back to the game of hockey.

Richard Desmond

Larry Ross

U.S. Navy Team (1942-1943)
St. Paul 7-Ups (1948-1950)
University of Minnesota (1950-1953)

Coach

Born: April 12, 1922, Duluth, Minn.

Larry Ross graduated from Duluth's Morgan Park High School, in 1940, where he starred between the pipes. He then entered the Navy and played on the Naval Team from 1942-43. From there Ross went on to star at the University of Minnesota, where he earned All-American honors in both 1951 and 1952.

Ross would go on to infamy, however, as the coach of International Falls High School, in extreme northern Minnesota. He led the Broncos to an amazing record of 566 wins, 169 losses and 21 ties. Over that time he also guided the squad to 13 State Tournaments, winning six State Championships. During one incredible stretch, from 1964-66, the Broncos went undefeated in 58 straight games.

Ross' players also swelled the ranks at all levels of college hockey, with eight playing Olympic Hockey, 12 playing in the National Hockey league, one player was a National Hockey League Linesman, while many went into coaching, refereeing as well.

In addition, while coaching at International Falls High School, he also started the hockey program at Rainy River Community College. He has received numerous honors and accolades, and even wrote a book entitled "Hockey For Everyone." He was later honored by his peers in 1983, when he was named Coach of the Year by the Minnesota Hockey Coaches Association. Then, in 1985, he was awarded the National High School Special Sports award by the National High School Athletic Coaches Association, while in 1988, he was the recipient of the John Mariucci College Award for his contribution to College Hockey by the American College Hockey Coaches Association.

After his retirement in 1985, Ross remained active in hockey, serving on the coaching staffs of various hockey schools in Minnesota. His 32 years as a coach can be best summed up by the words of another coaching legend, fellow Gopher classmate, "Badger" Bob Johnson, who stated, "He made a 100% Commitment to his job and the sport of hockey."

THE CLASS OF 1989

Roger A. Christian

United States National Team (1958-1965)
Olympic Team (1960-1964)
Warroad Lakers (1955-1974)

Wing

Born: December 1, 1935, Warroad, Minn.

Roger Christian began his early years in hockey like most other youngsters in Warroad, playing road hockey four to five hours or more on the river and on outdoor rinks. He and his brother, (fellow enshrinee) Billy, used magazines for shin pads and hockey sticks made by their father. They even shared a pair of skates and one would use them for half an hour then the other would trade.

Roger started playing high school hockey for Warroad in 1950, and by 1952 he was the team's leading scorer. In 1953 he led Warroad to the State Tournament, something scared to all kids in the Land of 10,000 Lakes. Over his storied prep career he was selected to the All-State Team, and was named All Region twice.

He would go on to star internationally after that. In 1958 he led the U.S. National team in scoring, under Coach Cal Marvin and Manager Don Clark, and in 1960 Roger played on the fabled Gold Medal winning Olympic Team, alongside his brother. He would go on to play on five U.S. National teams altogether.

After that Roger went on to play for nearly 20 years with his hometown Warroad Lakers, an amateur dynasty, where his No. 7 Jersey was later retired from the Laker's roster in 1974.

Roger later went on to co-found the multi-million dollar stick and equipment manufacturing company called Christian Brothers, where he continues to work today. In addition, he remains active in local community and youth hockey programs as well.

Roger Christian

Robert H. "Bob" Paradise

United States National Team (1969)
Olympic Team (1968)
Montreal Canadiens, Minnesota North Stars, Atlanta Flames, Pittsburgh Penguins and Washington Capitals (1969-79)

Defenseman

Born: April 22, 1944, St. Paul, Minn.

Bob Paradise

Robert Paradise began his interest in athletics, and hockey in particular, at the age of 10. He attended Cretin High School, where he starred in hockey, baseball, and football, earning all-state honors in hockey and football. From there he moved on to St. Mary's College in Winona, Minn., where he became an all-conference performer in the Minnesota Intercollegiate Athletic Conference for four consecutive years (first as a center and then as a defenseman).

It was at defense that the aggressive Paradise caught the eye of NFL scout and former Boston Bruins star, Fern Flaman. A well-rounded individual, Paradise even passed up an opportunity to sign a professional baseball contract with Boston Red Sox in 1965 in order to complete his education.

After graduation from St. Mary's in 1966, Paradise joined the 1968 United States Olympic Team, and later the 1969 National Team, before turning pro with the Montreal Canadiens organization.

After two years in the minors and brief stint with the North Stars, he was drafted by the Atlanta Flames in 1972, and then went on to a six-plus years career with the Flames, Pittsburgh, and Washington.

Paradise was a defensive-minded defenseman and at six-foot-one and 205 pounds, he was noted and respected for his physical style of play. He had to be tough. After all, he was the son-in-law of fellow Hall of Famer, Bob Dill, one of the toughest players ever to lace up the skates.

THE CLASS OF 1990

Herbert P. Brooks

Player: University of Minnesota (1955-59)
U.S. Olympic Teams (1964 and 1968)
(Forward and Defense)

Coach: University of Minnesota (1972-79); U.S. National Team (1979); U.S. Olympic Team (1980); New York Rangers (1981-85); St. Cloud State University (1986-87); Minnesota North Stars (1987-88).

Born: August 5, 1937, St. Paul, Minn.

Herb Brooks, is one of America's most celebrated coaches. The St. Paul "East Sider" got his first taste of championship hockey when he led his St. Paul Johnson squad to the Minnesota high school title in 1955. He would go on to play at the University of Minnesota for Coach John Mariucci, and then proceed to play on several U.S. National and Olympic teams from 1952-70.

Despite being an excellent skater, it was his innovative coaching that put him into the Hall of Fame. He took over at his alma mater in 1972, and led the last-place Gopher squad to an NCAA title just two years later. It would be the first of three crowns at the U of M for the coach, who would then go on to lead the fabled 1980 U.S. Olympic team to the "Miracle on Ice" gold medal.

From there Brooks entered the NHL coaching ranks, first with the New York Rangers, where, after three years, he was named Coach of the Year, and later with his hometown North Stars, in 1988. In between he even guided St. Cloud State (Minn.) for a year, bringing them up from Division III to Division I status.

Brooks went on to a successful business career which included motivational speaking, TV analysis, NHL scouting and occasional coaching. He even guided the French Olympic team in 1998. One of our nation's most charismatic and inventive coaches, "Herbie" is a true American hero.

Herb Brooks

Willard "Ike" Ikola

Player: Eveleth High School (1946-50)
University of Michigan (1951-54)
U.S. Olympic Team (1956)
U.S. National Teams (1957 & 1958)

Coach: Edina High School (1958-91)

Goaltender

Born: July 28, 1932, Eveleth, Minn.

Willard Ikola

With his now infamous hounds-toothed hat, "Ike" is best known throughout the Land of 10,000 Lakes for his amazing coaching record of 600-140-38 while at suburban Edina High School from 1958-91.

Ikola grew up as yet another in a long line of incredible goaltenders to come out of tiny Eveleth, Minnesota. Legends such as Frank Brimsek, Mike Karakas and Sam LoPresti, each Hall of Famers, were all heroes of Ikola. While he was fascinated by the heroic figures who preceded him in Eveleth, he more than lived up to the tradition.

As a freshman goalie, in 1947, Ikola's Golden Bears lost in the Minnesota state tournament semifinals. Incredibly, he never lost again, running off undefeated seasons to win titles in 1948, '49 and '50 as well.

From there, Ikola headed east, to attend the University of Michigan. After sitting out his freshman year, Ikola then led the Wolverines to the NCAA tournament the next three years, winning a pair of titles. In Ikola's sophomore year, Michigan beat Minnesota in the title game, while as a senior, and the only U.S. player on the roster, the Wolverines were upset by eventual champ RPI in the semifinals.

While serving in the military, Ikola played on the 1956 U.S. Olympic team in Cortina, Italy, which beat Germany ,7-2, upset Canada, 4-1, and beat Sweden, 6-1, before losing, 4-0, to the Soviet Union. A final 9-4 victory over Czechoslovakia then gave the U.S. the silver medal. He also played on U.S. National teams in 1957 and '58.

In the fall of 1958, Coach John Mariucci talked Edina High School into hiring Ikola on a trial basis as hockey coach. In his first year, Edina was 4-9-5. It would prove to be his only sub-.500 year over the next 33 seasons. After that, his guidance helped create one of the most cohesive youth development structures in the state, as his Edina "Hornets" went on to become a dynasty — winning a record eight state high school tournament titles.

John E. "Connie" Pleban

Played: Eveleth High School (1930-32)
Eveleth Junior College (1932-34)
Numerous Semi-pro teams.
U.S. National Team (1950)

Coached: U.S. Olympic team (1952); U.S. National teams (1950, 1961 and 1962); University of Minnesota-Duluth (1955-59); and numerous other amateur and semi-pro teams dating from 1936.

Born: April 24, 1914, Eveleth, Minn.

Connie Pleban

Connie Pleban played in the formative days of Northern Minnesota hockey, including Eveleth High School (1930-32) and Eveleth Junior College (1932-34). He played for the Babe Ruth national AAU champs in 1935, and was captain and later player-coach of the Eagle River, Wis., Falcons semipro team (1934-38). He was also player-coach with Eveleth Rangers semipro team (1938-41) and the Marquette, Mich., Sentinels semipro team (1941-42) before entering the service for World War II.

Returning to Eveleth, Pleban moved on as a coach and builder of amateur hockey serving as player-coach of the Eveleth Rangers again, and then holding the unique post of player-coach-manager of the U.S. National team that won the silver medal in London with a 4-1 record in 1950. Pleban was also named to reconstruct the U.S. fortunes for the 1952 Olympics as well. His team won the silver medal at Oslo, Norway, with a 6-1-1 record, losing only a 4-2 game to Sweden, while tying the gold medalists from Canada, 3-3.

In 1955, Pleban coached the University of Minnesota-Duluth, and helped lead its transition from small-college to major-college status. In his four-year tenure at UMD, Pleban's Bulldog teams never lost a game in the Minnesota Intercollegiate Athletic Conference. As a builder of the game, Pleban also successfully solicited NCAA rule-makers to expand body-checking from half to full ice — a move that would forever change the game.

Pleban went on to coach the U.S. team at the 1961 World Tournament in Geneva, to a 1-5-1 record. Then, in 1962, after only two preparatory games, he coached the U.S. to a much improved 5-2 record, which included winning the bronze medal at Colorado Springs.

A Duluth resident, Pleban also helped to organize amateur teams and leagues through the 1960s and '70s, always promoting and advancing the game every step of the way.

THE CLASS OF 1991

Robert "Robbie" Ftorek

U.S. Olympic Teams (1972)
U.S. National Teams (1976 and 1981)
Detroit Red Wings, NHL (1972-73), Quebec Nordiques, NHL (1980-81), New York Rangers, NHL (1982-85)
Phoenix and Cincinnati, WHA (1973-79)

Center

Born: January 1, 1952, Needham, Mass.

Inducted as an amateur, international and professional player, Robbie Ftorek grew up and went on to play high school hockey in Needham, Mass., where he was twice voted as the Massachusetts High School League MVP, and his teams won consecutive Eastern Massachusetts High School Titles in 1969 and 1970. Ftorek went on to play on Silver Medal-winning 1972 U.S. Olympic Team, while later playing on the 1976 and 1981 US/Canada Cup teams.

He made the jump to play pro hockey in 1972, with the Detroit Red Wings, and later in the WHA, where he was the first American developed player to be named league MVP in 1977. In five seasons, three with Phoenix and two with Cincinnati, the speedy center scored 40 or more goals three times and passed the 100 point mark on four occasions. Named to the all-league first team twice, in 1979 he scored 59 goals, tying the record with Joe Mullen for most goals scored by an American-developed player in a professional league.

In 1980 Ftorek served as the Team Captain at Quebec, then only the second American developed player to hold that title in the NHL. He later played with the New York Rangers from 1982-85, and then got into coaching, where, in 1987 he took over as the Head Coach of the LA Kings. He later joined the New Jersey Devils coaching staff in 1992 and took over as head coach there in 1998 as well.

Robbie Ftorek

Robert "Bob" Johnson

NCAA: Colorado College (1963-66)
University of Wisconsin (1966-81)

NHL: Calgary Flames (1982-87)
Pittsburgh Penguins (1990-91)

Several U.S. Olympic and National Teams

Inducted as Coach/Administrator

Born: 1931, Minneapolis, Minn.

"Badger" Bob Johnson

Minneapolis native Bob Johnson, a graduate of Minneapolis Central High School, went on to play left wing for the Gopher Hockey team from 1954-55 under legendary Coach John Mariucci. Following a couple of high school coaching stints at both Warroad (Minn.) and Minneapolis Roosevelt, where he won four City Conference championships in six years, he took over the reins at Colorado College in 1963.

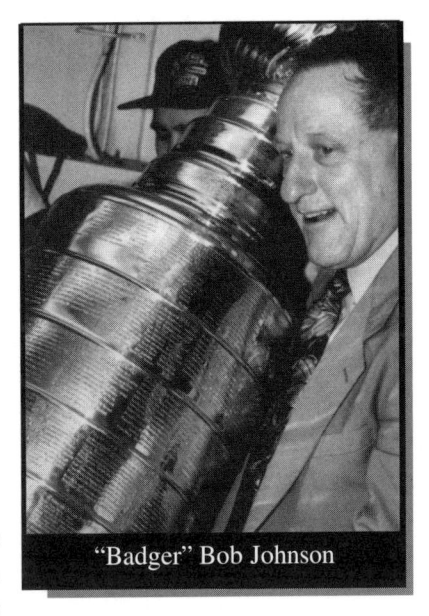

After several years at C.C., he moved to the University of Wisconsin, where, in a period of 11 years, he led the Badgers to seven NCAA tournaments, winning three championships and one second-place finish. It was there where the 1977 NCAA Coach of the Year recipient was given the nickname, "Badger Bob."

He also led the 1976 U.S. Olympic team to a fourth-place finish at Innsbruck, Austria, and coached the 1981, 1984, and 1987 U.S. teams in the Canada Cup as well. In addition, he coached the 1973, 1974, 1975, and 1981 U.S. National Teams.

Beginning in 1982 Johnson coached the NHL's Calgary Flames for five seasons. In 1990 he took over as coach of the Pittsburgh Penguins, where in his first season, he led the team, which was led by superstar Mario Lemieux, to a Stanley Cup victory over his hometown Minnesota North Stars, four games to two.

A tireless promoter of American hockey, Johnson also served as Executive Director of USA Hockey for a three-year period in the 1980s. Then, in November of 1991, Johnson tragically died of brain cancer at the age of 60. Bob Johnson's memory lives on forever, however, from his now-famous phrase which epitomized his love for the game: "It's a great day for hockey."

Described as driven, compulsive and tenacious, Badger Bob was one of the greatest hockey coaches ever to hail from Minnesota. He was later inducted into the Hockey Hall of Fame, in Toronto, in 1992.

John Matchefts

Player: University of Michigan (1951-53)
U.S. National Team (1951)
U.S. Olympic Team (1952)

Center - Left Wing

Coach: Colorado College (1966-71)
Air Force Academy (1972-86)

Born: June 18, 1931, Eveleth, Minn.

John Matchefts

John Matchefts grew up loving the game of hockey in his hometown of Eveleth, Minnesota. There, the speedy youngster first learned how to skate by borrowing his big sister's figure skates. Then, in 1948, at the age of 16, Matchefts emerged as a high school star for the Eveleth Golden Bears. There, under fellow enshrinee, Coach Cliff Thompson, he quickly became a phenome. So good was the lightning-quick winger, that he was even invited to play for the 1948 U.S. Olympic team. While high school league rules prevented him from playing that year, he did later represent his country at the World Championships in 1955, and again in 1956, where he won a silver medal on the Olympic team.

Matchefts was a prep star at Eveleth. Teaming up with another enshrinee, John Mayasich, he not only led the Golden Bears to three straight undefeated state hockey championships from 1947-49, he also excelled at football and baseball as well. In fact, he was the first player named to the all-State high school hockey team three times.

From there he decided to attend the University of Michigan, where the two-time All-American and team captain led the Wolverines to three straight NCAA hockey championships, from 1951-53. Nicknamed "the Fly" because of his amazing speed and maneuverability, Matchefts averaged two points per game, with 57 goals and 74 assists over his college career.

After his collegiate playing days, Matchefts declined the opportunity to play professional hockey, and instead played on the 1955 and '56 U.S. National and Olympic teams. From there he went on to spend more than a decade as a high school hockey coach in Eveleth and Thief River Falls, where he guided several of his teams from both schools to the state's fabled high school tournament.

Matchefts made the jump to big-time coaching after that, as he later took over behind the bench at Colorado College, from 1966-71, and at the Air Force Academy, from 1972-86. Among his many honors and accolades, he was named as the WCHA's Coach of the Year in 1968.

THE CLASS OF 1992

Amo Bessone

Coach: Michigan State University (1951-1979)
       Michigan Tech University (1948-50)

Born: November 22, 1916, Sagamore, Mass.

For 28 years, Amo Bessone was known as much as a father figure as he was a hockey coach at Michigan State University. Bessone, who coached three seasons at Michigan Tech before moving to East Lansing in 1951, was one of the most prominent leaders in the days when college hockey was organized, operated and regulated by the coaches.

Building Michigan State hockey was an arduous task. The Spartans endured 18 seasons in league play before rising above the .500 mark, but he tried to recruit the top regional U.S. players in those years against dominant foes. Bessone's lifetime 367-427-20 record, doesn't accurately reflect his teams' competitiveness. His perseverance was rewarded in the 1966 season when his Cinderella Spartans won the NCAA Championship. A year later, after placing fifth with an 8-11-1 WCHA record, Amo's Spartans nearly did it again, reaching the NCAA Final Four before losing in the semifinals.

Bessone's colorful, cigar-chomping coaching career obscures what was also an impressive playing career. Growing up in Springfield, Mass., in the 1920's, Bessone played on the Old Bed pond at the Exposition Grounds with his older brother, Pete — also a Hall of Fame inductee. Amo went on to play defense at West Springfield High School, Kent's Hill and Hebron Academies in Maine, and also the University of Illinois.

He played pro hockey, briefly, for the Detroit Wings in 1936, and later with Springfield in the American League, taking time out to be skipper of PT boat in World War II. After the war, Bessone coached hockey and assisted with football and baseball at Westfield High School, in Massachusetts, before starting Michigan Tech's hockey program in 1948.

Amo Bessone

Len Ceglarski

Coach: Clarkson College (1958-72)
Boston College (1972-92)

Born: June 27, 1926, East Walpole, Mass.

Becoming a legend is no easy task, but Ceglarski's status was legendary long before he resigned as Boston College Coach at the end of the 1992 season. He set the record for most coaching victories in college hockey, with 673 triumphs over his 34-year career, and he is the only coach to ever have more than 250 victories at two different colleges.

At Clarkson, where Ceglarski began coaching in 1958, the Knights rolled up a 254-97-10 record in 14 seasons, with one ECAC championship, 11 consecutive trips to the ECAC tournament, and four to the NCAA tournament. His Clarkson teams won over 20 games six times, and three of his teams lost in NCAA title games — the 1962 team, which was 22-3-1; the 1966 team, which was 24-3; and the 1970 team, which was 24-8.

Then, in 1972, Ceglarski moved to Boston College, his alma mater, where he replaced his old coach, Hall of Famer John "Snooks" Kelley, who was the first college coach to ever win 500 games. Ceglarski maintained that tradition and became the first college coach to win 600 games. Ceglarski won his first of three Spencer Penrose Awards as the nation's top college coach when his first Boston College team won the ECAC tournament and went to the NCAA Final Four. In 20 seasons, Ceglarski's Eagles posted a 419-242-27 record, first winning the ECAC title in 1978, then, when Hockey East began in the 1985 season, winning six of the first seven league championships. His Eagles team won over 20 games 11 times, including a Boston College record 31-8 season in 1987, and made nine more trips to the CCAA tournament.

The NCAA title Ceglarski strived for as coach, he attained as a player. As a sophomore, Ceglarski scored the tying goal in the 4-3 NCAA Championship game won by Boston College over Dartmouth in 1949. Ceglarski was All-American as a junior, team captain as a senior, and ranked fourth on Boston College's all-time scoring list with 49-59-108 in only 52 games. He also lettered three times in baseball as well. Ceglarski later played on the silver medal 1952 US Olympic team, served in the Marine Corps, then returned to the Boston Area to began coaching at Norwood and Walpole high schools, winning the New England Championship with Walpole in 1958. Len and his wife, Ursula, had six sons, while Tim, the youngest, played for Dad at Boston College.

James Fullerton

Brown University (1955-72)

Coach

Born: April 9, 1909, Mass.

One of the true gentlemen in the sport, Jim Fullerton became the first full-time coach at Brown University in 1955. In his early years, he sometimes had trouble filling out a roster at the Ivy League school known more for its academics than its athletics. But in the span of a decade, he had generated the evolution of a strong, substantial hockey program.

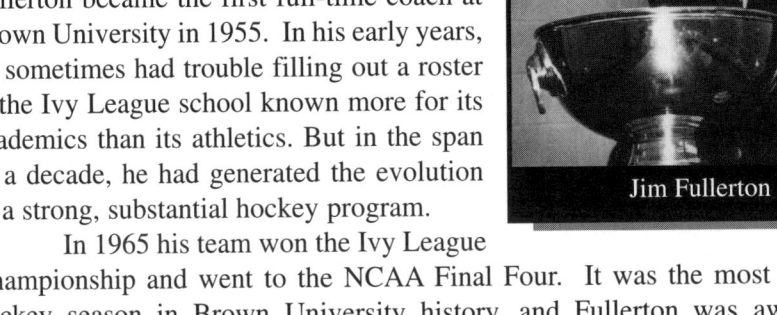

In 1965 his team won the Ivy League Championship and went to the NCAA Final Four. It was the most successful hockey season in Brown University history, and Fullerton was awarded the Spencer Penrose Award as the nation's coach of the year.

In 15 seasons, his Brown teams gave him a lifetime coaching record of 176-168-9. Fullerton ran a classy, first-rate operation at Brown, and his fellow coaches recognized his outstanding coaching ability. He was a four-time recipient of the New England Coach of the Year (the Clark Hodder Award), was named to the U.S. Collegiate Hall of Fame in 1971 and Brown University's Hall of Fame in 1974.

Fullerton also coached the US team for the World Games against the Soviet Union and Canada in 1972. In addition, he was a member of the US Olympic Committee for the World Games against the Soviet Union and Canada that same year as well. A member of the US Olympic Committee from 1969-72, he later scouted for the Chicago Blackhawks and the New York Islanders.

As a player, Fullerton starred at Norwich University but turned down the opportunity to play pro in order to accept a coaching job at Norwood. He would remain there for 24 years, bringing that school solid recognition as a formidable hockey power and sending numerous players off to collegiate careers.

Beyond that, Fullerton also worked as a top hockey official. From 1933-55, Fullerton refereed professional, college and high school games in the Lake Placid area. He became vice-president of the New England Chapter of the AAU referees and was referee-in-chief for the 1939 national amateur championships in Lake Placid. When he accepted the challenge to move to Brown, Fullerton continued to show his organizational skills as a prominent force in the formation and development of the American Hockey Coaches Association, which he also served as president.

THE CLASS OF 1993

John "Snooks" Kelley

Coach: Boston College (1936-1972)

Born: July 11, 1907, Cambridge, Mass.

"Snooks" Kelley grew up loving hockey and went on to become a star player for Cambridge Latin and Dean Academy before enrolling at Boston College. There, from 1928-30, he emerged as the Eagles top player, graduating in 1930, just after the stock market had wiped out hockey as a varsity sport.

On January 8, 1933 he agreed to coach a group of BC students. The job was part-time and without pay, complementing his teaching at Cambridge Latin. He gave up playing the game with the Boston Hockey Club at that time to begin an unprecedented stint, broken only by the war years of 1942-46, when he served in the Navy. Snooks' career reached a high point in March of 1949 when his Eagles won the NCAA title, defeating fellow Hall of Fame enshrinee Eddie Jeremiah's Dartmouth team, 4-3.

In all, Kelley's teams were invited to the NCAA Tournament nine times, more than any other Eastern team. They were the first Eastern team to win the title in a series that had been dominated by teams from the West. Over the years, teams under Kelley traveled more than 80,000 miles on road trips, spreading the gospel of college hockey for American youth. He steadfastly refused to recruit players from Canada because he felt that to do so would deprive American boys of a chance to develop their hockey potential in elite competition.

Other accomplishments included eight New England Championships, nine appearances in the ECAC Division I playoffs, one ECAC playoff crown, and eight Beanpot Tournament titles. In 1959 and 1972 he received the Spencer Penrose Award as College Hockey's Coach of the Year. In addition, 16 of his players won All-American honors while several went on to play for U.S. Olympic and National Teams. Topping it all off was Coach Kelley's career record of 501 victories, 242 losses, and 15 ties.

Snooks Kelley

Dave Langevin

New York Islanders

Defense

Born: May 15, 1954, St. Paul, Minn.

A rangy, mobile defenseman, Dave Langevin is best known for winning four Stanley Cup rings as a member of the New York Islanders from 1979 to 1985. But Langevin's career was characterized by success wherever he played.

A graduate of St. Paul's Hazel Park playground, Langevin went on to star at Hill High School (later Hill-Murray), where he played on two state independent championship teams, helping compile a 28-1 record his junior year.

From there he went on to star at the University of Minnesota-Duluth, where he emerged as one of the team's star players from 1972-76. He patrolled the Bulldog blue lines with authority and was named as a second-team All American after his senior year.

His first professional experience came with the Edmonton Oilers in the old World Hockey Association, which Langevin considered a great opportunity for budding U.S. professional players. After three seasons the league folded, and he wound up with the Islanders. It would be the break of a lifetime, as his first four seasons in the National Hockey League, 1980-83, were all climaxed by Stanley Cup triumphs.

"It was hard to say how great our team was while being part of it", Langevin recalled. "All I know is that our practices were a lot harder than a lot of our games."

In 1982 he represented the United States by playing with Team USA in the Canada Cup series. Then, after a devastating knee injury, which nearly ended his career, sidelined him, he worked hard to rehabilitate himself back into game shape. Told he'd never play again before the Islanders fourth Stanley Cup bid, Langevin came back to star in the four-game sweep over former Oilers teammates that included Wayne Gretzky. Langevin, who earned All-Star honors in 1983, later played a season with the Minnesota North Stars and ended his career with the Los Angeles Kings. There, after reinjuring his knee, he opted to retire at the age of 33.

Langevin later pursued a coaching career in high school, amateur, and college hockey while residing in St. Paul with his family.

Charles M. Schulz

Charles Schulz

Builder and No. 1 Fan

Born: Nov. 26, 1922, Minneapolis, Minn.

"Good Grief!" Here's a world-famous hockey player, Snoopy, taking on Woodstock on a frozen birdbath. Here's the world-famous "Peanuts" cartoonist, arena-builder, and organizer of "Snoopy's Senior Hockey Tournament." Charles Schulz, going into the U.S. Hockey Hall of Fame.

Growing up in St. Paul, Schulz shot tennis balls in his grandmother's basement, coaxed his mother to make goalie pads out of gunny sacks with rolled-up newspaper sewn inside, and was enthralled when his parents took him to St. Paul Saints and Minneapolis Millers games in the 1930s. His father made a rink in the family's backyard, and Schulz and his friends even played by lamplight on frozen streets or neighborhood school rinks.

After graduating from St. Paul Central High, Schulz went on to art school in Minneapolis. There, he created a comic strip about the adventures of a group of preschoolers (including a kid named Charlie Brown) called "Li'l Folks," which appeared in the St. Paul Pioneer Press in 1947. United Features Syndicate bought the strip in 1950 and renamed it "Peanuts" because 'Li'l Folks" sounded too much like another cartoon, "Li'l Abner." Seven newspapers carried the original "Peanuts" strip on October 2, 1950, and the numbers have grown ever since.

He later moved on to California, where he became one of the world most famous cartoonists. The multiple Emmy winner's cartoons are now read by several hundred million people in 68 countries, who speak 26 different languages.

All the while, his love for hockey traveled with him when his cartooning career led him to the West Coast. Schulz's five children learned to skate at the only arena in the Santa Rosa area. When the arena closed, Schulz's first wife, Joyce, convinced him to build the Redwood Empire Arena near his studio in 1969.

Supported by his second wife, Jeannie, Schulz started a senior hockey tournament at his arena in the early 1970s. The tournament soon became more than a place for Schulz to demonstrate his "off-wing" style as a forward. From a dozen first-year teams, it has grown into the world's largest senior hockey tournament. In 1993, 188 "over-40" teams applied for the 56 spots. A unique "over-70" bracket with four teams was also added. "They were just waiting for me to turn 70," Schulz joked. Schulz was also honored in 1981 by winning the Lester Patrick Award for outstanding service to hockey.

THE CLASS OF 1994

Joseph Cavanagh, Jr.

Harvard University (1968-70)
Forward
Born: April 13, 1948, Providence, RI

Known as one of the greatest prep hockey players in New England history, Joe Cavanagh was raised in a family of eight children in Warwick, Rhode Island. A talented forward who was reknowned for his hard work on the ice, Cavanagh was a three-time all-state selection for the Thunderbolts, as he led the state in scoring during the 1964, '65 and '66 seasons. He was also named Rhode Island's most valuable high school player in '65 and '66. As a collegian, Cavanagh skated for Harvard for three seasons (freshmen were not allowed to participate in varsity athletics under the NCAA rules of the time). His sophomore season of 1969 saw him make a big impression during his first foray into college hockey. Incredibly, he was selected as a first team all-American, first team All-East, first team All-Ivy, first team All-New England, was named as the recipient of the Walter Brown Award (given to best American-born player), and was named most valuable player of the annual Beanpot tournament — which the Crimson won by beating Boston University. After his junior and senior seasons with the Crimson, Cavanagh was again named to the first team All-American, All-East, All-Ivy and All-New England squads, and he won the Walter Brown Award again during his final season at Harvard. He was the team's leading scorer all three seasons (tied with Robert McNamara as a junior), and was also given the John Tudor Memorial Cup Award as team most valuable player after his junior and senior seasons. When it was all said and done, he ranked fifth on the Crimson all-time scoring list with 60 goals and 127 assists. His 50 assists during his senior season still stands as a Crimson record.

"He was a great player with outstanding talent, and I've never seen a player work as hard on the rink as Joey did — which not all outstanding players do," said Hall of Famer Bill Cleary, who coached Cavanagh at Harvard. "Work ethic was as much a part of the package as talent."

Cavanagh, who was named to the Eastern Collegiate Athletic Conference's All Decade first team for his efforts on the ice, went on to coach youth hockey in his hometown in 1982, later serving on the Warwick Junior Hockey Association's board of directors. Cavanagh, an attorney in the Warwick area, and his wife Carol raised eight children.

Joe Cavanagh Jr.

Wally Grant

University of Michigan (1946-50)

Forward

Born: December 8, 1927, Leonidas, Minn.

Wally Grant got his start in hockey on the Iron Range of northeastern Minnesota. Best known for the high school and collegiate championships, he went on to star at both Eveleth High School (Minn.), and later at the University of Michigan.

Grant was a participant in the first ever Minnesota State High School Hockey Tournament in 1945, and played a major role in the Golden Bears winning the inaugural title under legendary coach and fellow enshrinee Cliff Thompson. Trailing Thief River Falls in the championship game, Grant scored the Bears' third and fourth goals as Eveleth came back to win 4-3. Playing on a line with Pat Finnigan and Neil Celley, Grant established a high school playoff record with 13 points. That record remained one of the top five performances in state history for more than four decades.

From Eveleth, Grant moved on to the University of Michigan, where his team participated in the first NCAA Ice Hockey Championship, in 1948. Coached by Vic Heyliger, the Wolverines defeated Dartmouth 8-4 in the title game to claim the first ever title. Grant also starred as a member of Michigan's infamous "G" line, which included Wally Gacek and Ted Greer. Each of the three linemates scored a third-period goal in Michigan's championship win. He played four seasons for Michigan between 1946 and 1950, participating in the NCAA tournament in three of those seasons. He took one season off after his freshman year to serve in the U.S. Military.

He was never a big player, but made up for it with speed and quickness. "I was 5'8 and 165 pounds, but I was fast enough to get around some of those defensemen," he said. "That was my advantage."

Grant went on to work for General Motors in Michigan for 37 years before finally retiring in the late 1980s. Still following his alma mater, Grant served as vice president of the Dekers Blue Line Club — a Michigan hockey booster organization, as well as being a part of the Graduate "M" Club and Michigan's Victors Club. He and wife Ellen raised three children in the Ann Arbor area.

Ned Harkness

RPI, Cornell University & Union College

Coach

Born: September 19, 1921, Ottawa, Canada

Ned Harkness

Remembered as one of American hockey's true founding fathers, Ned Harkness established and served hockey programs, organizations and facilities on many levels for more than four decades. Born in Ontario, Harkness became a naturalized American citizen in 1949. One year later he founded the varsity hockey program at Troy, New York's, Rensselaer Polytechnic Institute and guided the Engineers to an NCAA championship within the program's first half-decade. Harkness coached RPI to a 5-4 overtime win over Minnesota in the 1954 national championship game and led his Engineers to the Eastern championship in 1961.

In 1963, Harkness took over the coaching reins at Cornell, and launched the Big Red on a memorable string of successes. Under his guidance, Cornell won NCAA titles in 1967 and 1970, while finishing second in 1969 and third in 1968. He was also named national coach of the year in '68 as well. During his eight seasons behind the Big Red bench, Harkness' teams also won five Ivy League titles and four Eastern championships. In addition, the 1970 championship team set a mark that will never be eclipsed, finishing the season with a 29-0 record-the finest win-loss mark in the history of NCAA Division I hockey.

From Cornell, Harkness was appointed coach of the National Hockey League's Detroit Red Wings, making him the first coach to go from the American college ranks to the NHL. He spent four seasons in the Detroit organization, first as head coach and later as general manager. Harkness then established a hockey program at Schenectady, New York's Union College, and served as coach and rink director for the Skating Dutchmen until 1977. A year later he supervised construction on the Glens Falls (New York) Civic Center and founded the Adirondack Red Wings of the American Hockey League in 1979, serving as their general manager. For his efforts with the Red Wings, Harkness was named the AHL's executive of the year in 1980, and was given the Daoust Golden Skate Award in 1986 for contributions to the AHL.

In 1982, Harkness was appointed president and chief executive officer of the U.S. Olympic Regional Development Authority in Lake Placid, New York. He is a member of halls of fame for Cornell, New York State, Glens Falls and RPI.

THE CLASS OF 1995

Henry Boucha

U.S. Olympic Team (1972), Detroit Red Wings (1972-74), Minnesota North Stars (1975), Minnesota Fighting Saints (WHA) (1976), KC Scouts (1976) and Colorado Rockies (1977)

Wing

Born: June 1, 1951, Warroad, Minn.

Henry Boucha has been labeled as the most electrifying player in Minnesota hockey history. Also skilled in football and baseball, Boucha starred for five years at both defense and center for the Warroad High School hockey team. A tall, powerfully-built Ojibwe Indian, Boucha led Warroad to the 1969 state tournament, where he was injured in an emotionally-charged 5-4 overtime final loss to Edina — one of the all-time classic games in "tourney" history.

"He was the most colorful hockey player ever to come out of Northern Minnesota," said Warroad coaching legend and fellow Hall of Fame enshrinee Cal Marvin. "When he played, it was so special that he brought people out of the old folks home to come and watch him play. He did it all. He was one of a kind."

Boucha went on to play for the 1972 silver medal winning U.S. Olympic team, and at just 19, he signed with the Detroit Red Wings. After two years in the Motor City, Boucha "came home" when the Minnesota North Stars acquired him. But his career was tragically curtailed in his third NHL season when he suffered an eye injury on Jan. 4, 1975 against Boston.

He would come back to play for the WHA's Minnesota Fighting Saints in 1976, and then again in 1977 with the Scouts and Rockies of the NHL, but couldn't overcome his eye injury. He retired from the game after that at just the age of 24.

Boucha would go on to play for his hometown Warroad Lakers, and then give back by donating much of his time to helping advance various Native American causes.

Henry Boucha

James Claypool

1960 U.S. Olympic Team

Manager/Administrator

Born: July 19, 1921, Hibbing, Minn.

True dedication as a hockey administrator was defined by Claypool when, after managing the 1960 U.S. Olympic hockey team that won the Gold Medal at Squaw Valley, California, he returned to his family in Duluth, Minnesota and renewed his involvement in youth hockey, managing the 1965 Peewee team that won the national championship.

Jim Claypool

Jim Claypool grew up in Hibbing, Minn., playing hockey. After his sophomore year, he then moved on to attend prep school in Pennsylvania, where he continued to play the game he loved. From there the winger went on to attend the University of Michigan, where, from 1941-42, he starred for the Wolverines. His college career was interrupted in 1943, when he was asked to serve his country in World War II as a member of the Navy.

Upon his return home, he moved back to his native Minnesota. There, he settled down in Duluth, where, in addition to beginning his career in the banking industry, his love of the game had him managing the local semi-pro Duluth Coolerator's as well. In 1947 he also became a U.S. Delegate for the Ice Hockey Federation, maintaining his involvement with at the administrative level of the game. In addition, he later served as the President of the Duluth Amateur Hockey Association.

While raising a family, Claypool helped coordinate the building of neighborhood rinks and hockey programs, and became president of the Minnesota Amateur Hockey Association in 1957. He remained very active in the politics and in policy-making throughout that era, always bettering the game for kids across America.

After returning from the Olympics in Squaw Valley, Claypool went on to become the President of 1st Bank of Duluth. As a respected businessman and hockey administrator, he found a way to get things done.

In the 1970's he coordinated the construction of indoor arenas in Duluth, where the strength of youth and high school hockey continues to reflect his efforts. Jim Claypool was a true friend to hockey, not only in Minnesota, but throughout the United States.

Ken Morrow

United States Olympic Team (1980)
New York Islanders (1980-89)

Defenseman

Born: October 17, 1956, Flint, Mich.

A magical three-month span in the spring of 1980 assured Ken Morrow of a place in hockey history. The giant, 6-4, 205 pound defenseman played an integral role on the fabled U.S. Olympic hockey team that won the Gold Medal at Lake Placid in February of 1980.

Morrow grew up playing hockey in Michigan, and went on to star in college at Bowling Green. There he was the first All-American ever chosen at the school, and was named as the CCHA player of the year in 1979. In addition to garnering CCHA first-team honors in 1976, '78 and '79, he also earned All-American honors in 1978 as well.

He also played on the U.S. National teams in both 1978 and '79 before being selected to play for Herb Brooks and the "Miracle on Ice" Olympic team in 1980.

From there Morrow made the leap to the big-time, signing on with the New York Islanders, where he continued to stand out on a team that won the Stanley Cup in May — beating the Minnesota North Stars four games to one. While becoming the only player ever to win both an Olympic Gold Medal and a Stanley Cup in the same year, Morrow and the Islanders would go on to earn four consecutive Stanley Cups. Morrow played sturdy defense all along as well, as the team proved to be one of the NHL's best ever throughout the decade of the 1980s.

One of his personal highlights came in the 1984 playoffs, when he scored the overtime game-winner in the deciding contest against the Rangers. For his NHL career, the tough defenseman scored 17 goals and 88 assists for 105 points in 550 games played.

Morrow continued to give back to the game even after his retirement, and in 1996 was awarded the Lester Patrick Trophy for his efforts.

THE CLASS OF 1996

Sergio "Serge" Gambucci

Coach
Born: January 11, 1923, Eveleth, Minn.

Sergio "Serge" Gambucci crafted a legendary hockey career out of two basic ingredients: A love for the game of hockey and a conviction that invaluable life lessons could be taught and learned through athletic competition.

Gambucci's career started in his native Eveleth, MN., where his athletic prowess brought him national recognition. His career was interrupted after high school when he was called into military service during World War II. Upon his return, he attended St. Cloud Teachers College (now St. Cloud State University), where he captained the hockey team and was its leading scorer for two years.

Serge then continued to play top-level amateur hockey after college. In 1951, he was player-coach and leading scorer for the Crookston Pirates, that year's U.S. amateur national champion. After that however, Serge chose to dedicate his career to teaching and coaching. First at Cathedral High School in Crookston, MN., then at Central High School in Grand Forks, ND., Gambucci fashioned a record marked by success on the ice and the admiration, gratitude and friendship of his players long after their playing careers ended. His Grand Forks Central teams won 10 consecutive North Dakota state championships between 1961 and 1970, and he finished his coaching career with the third highest winning percentage in U.S. high school hockey history.

Serge Gambucci's lifetime achievements have been recognized by his peers through his induction into several Halls of Fame, including: the Grand Forks Central Athletic , the Grand Forks Public School Teachers, the St. Cloud University and the North Dakota Coaches Association. Upon his retirement, Gambucci was recognized on the floor of the U.S. Senate by Sen. Kent Conrad, who said, "As a teacher and a role model, he inspired thousands of students with a message of integrity and hard work." Serge and his wife, Eleanor, have seven children and many grandchildren.

Serge Gambucci

Reed Larson

Detroit Red Wings (1976-86)
Boston Bruins (1986-88)
Edmonton Oilers, New York Islanders, North Stars and Buffalo Sabres (1988-90)

Defenseman

Born: July 30, 1956, Minneapolis, Minn.

Reed Larson came out of the park board and youth hockey programs of Minneapolis in the 1960's and into a career that included more than 900 games in the National Hockey League, as one of the steadiest defensemen in the era.

Reed Larson

Larson's playing career included 14 seasons in the NHL, during which he played in three NHL All-Star Games. He served as captain of the Detroit Red Wings from 1982-86, and helped guide the Boston Bruins to the 1986 Stanley Cup Finals. All along the way, he was the epitome of professionalism and dedication. He finished his NHL career with a total of 222 goals and 463 assists for 685 points in 904 games.

Reed was born in south Minneapolis and played on his first hockey team at the age of six at Sibley Park. He went on to star at Roosevelt High School, where he was named all-city and all-state both his junior and senior years. It was then on to the University of Minnesota, where, under Coach Herb Brooks, Larson was a key factor as the Gophers captured the 1975 WCHA championship, finished as NCAA runner-up in 1975, then captured the NCAA title in 1976.

Larson turned professional in the middle of his junior year, signing with the Detroit Red Wings, who had drafted him in the second round. He was the runner-up in voting for NHL Rookie of the Year. After nearly a decade with the Red Wings, Reed was traded to Boston, where he played for another two and a half seasons. He finished his NHL career with stints for the Edmonton Oilers, New York Islanders, Minnesota North Stars and Buffalo Sabres. But he wasn't through with pro hockey. He moved to Italy and was a standout in the Italian professional league for five seasons, totaling 65 goals and 150 assists for 215 points in 159 games.

A highlight of Reed's career was playing in both the World Championships and the Canada Cup in 1981, representing the United States. Larson remains as one of Minnesota's greatest ever hockey heroes, and remains active in the local Twin Cities community as both a role-model to aspiring youngsters out on the ice and also as an insurance executive.

Craig Patrick

California Golden Seals (1971-75)
St. Louis Blues (1975)
Kansas City Scouts (1976)
Washington Capitals (1976-79)
Minnesota Fighting Saints (WHA) (1977)
U.S. National Teams (1969-71, 1977 & '79)
U.S. Olympic Team (1980) (Administrator)
New York Rangers (1980-86) GM
Pittsburgh Penguins (1988-Present)

Wing

Born: May 20, 1946, Detroit, Mich.

A graduate of the University of Denver, Craig Patrick helped the Pioneers to NCAA Hockey Championships in 1968 and 1969. From there the speedy winger went on to spend eight years in the NHL with California, St. Louis, Kansas City and Washington and played one season with Minnesota of the WHA before retiring in 1979. Over his eight-year NHL career he scored 91 goals and 72 assists for 163 total points.

He also served as captain for Team USA in the 1979 World Champions in Moscow and played on the 1976 US Canada Cup team. Patrick also became a part of sports history that Americans will long remember when he served as assistant general manager and assistant coach of the 1980 gold medal U.S. Olympic hockey team in Lake Placid.

He joined the New York Rangers as director of operations in 1980 and in 1981 became the youngest general manager in their history. Serving in that capacity through the 1986 season, his team gained the playoffs every year. As general manager of the Pittsburgh Penguins, his team won back-to-back Stanley Cups in 1991 and 1992 and have been continuous contenders in ensuing years. He has since become the longest-serving GM in franchise history and twice during his tenure he took over behind the bench, coaching the team briefly in 1990 and 1997. In 1999 he even hired his old 1980 Olympic Team boss, Herb Brooks, to take over as the team's head coach — a position Herbie would relinquish after that season.

One of the game's brightest minds, Patrick comes from some pretty good hockey lineage. He is the son of Hall of Famer Lynn Patrick and the grandson of of hockey legend Lester Patrick. In addition, his uncle, Muzz Patrick was also an NHL star and later an executive with the Rangers as well. His cousin, Dick Patrick was an executive with the Washington Capitals, and Craig's brother, Frank, is also a member of the Hall of Fame in Toronto.

THE CLASS OF 1997

Charles "Charlie" Holt

Colby College (1962-68)
University of New Hampshire (1968-86)

Coach

Born: July 17, 1922

Considered a legend in the college coaching ranks, Charlie Holt began his college coaching career in 1962 at Colby College. There he racked up 65 victories, and turned the school's hockey program around. Then, in 1968 he took the head coaching job at the University of New Hampshire, where he remained for 18 seasons. Under Holt's leadership, New Hampshire qualified for the ECAC playoffs 14 of his 18 seasons, played in the NCAA Division I Final Four three times — 1977, 1979 and 1982 — and accumulated a 347-232 win-loss record.

The winner of the Spence Penrose College Coach of the Year Award on three different occasions, Holt's tribute is best stated by fellow Hall of Famer Bill Cleary, who said, "Charlie Holt's contributions to college hockey have been extraordinary as a coach and as an innovator. His legacy is the many he coached who are now included in hockey as coaches and administrators."

Charlie is a true friend to the game of hockey, and has contributed to the advancement to the game on many levels.

"Charlie Holt's achievements as a superb and universally respected hockey coach at UNH are well known," said UNH President Joan Leitzel at the time of Holt's death in March of 2000. "In addition, he left a great legacy on the ways student-athletes, coaches and citizens, in general, should conduct themselves and treat one another. His high ideals for perfection, professionalism, mutual respect, discipline and excellence will always be remembered and he will continue to serve as a role model for us and posterity."

Holt is survived by his wife, Nancy, and his children, Brad and Brenda.

Bill Nyrop

Montreal Canadiens (1975-78)
Minnesota North Stars (1981-82)
United States National Team (1977)

Defenseman

Born: July 23, 1952, Washington D.C.

An outstanding defenseman, Bill Nyrop reached the top in all phases of hockey as a player. He was an outstanding athlete at Edina (Minn.) High School, where he led his Hornets to a state championship in 1969 over fellow enshrinee Henry Boucha's Warroad Warriors in the title game. He was also an All-State selection that year as well.

From there Nyrop enrolled at the University of Notre Dame, where he played from 1970-74. The defenseman tallied 99 points during his tenure for the Fighting Irish and earned All-American honors in 1973.

In 1972 Nyrop was selected as the 66th player in the NHL entry draft by the Montreal Canadiens. After his illustrious collegiate career, he was assigned to Nova Scotia of the American Hockey League, where he played for two seasons. In 1976 Nyrop was elevated to the parent team in Montreal, where he played for three consecutive Stanley Cup championship teams and was selected as a 1978 NHL All Star.

Nyrop then retired in 1979 to pursue a law degree, but was persuaded to play one more NHL season with the Minnesota North Stars in 1981. Upon playing for one more season in Germany, he hung em' up for good, finishing his NHL career with 63 points.

After getting his law degree, Nyrop returned to hockey in 1992 as the general manager of the Knoxville (Tenn.) East Coast Hockey League club. In addition, he later founded the West Palm Beach (Fla.) team in the Sunshine Hockey League.

Then, tragically, the hockey world was shocked when Bill Nyrop died of cancer at the age of 43. Always a remarkable, physical specimen, he became ill in August of 1995 and passed away four months later on December 31, 1995. He was truly one of the good guys.

Timothy Sheehy

New England Whalers (WHA) (1972-75, '78)
Edmonton (1975-77)
Birmingham (1977)
Detroit Red Wings (1978)
Hartford (1979-80)

Winger

Born: September 3, 1948, Fort Frances, Ont.

Tim Sheehy is a native of International Falls, Minn., where he led his high school team to three consecutive state championships and 59 straight wins from 1964-66.

Tim Sheehy

Presented with the opportunity to play major junior hockey in Canada as an NHL No. 1 draft pick, Sheehy declined, deciding instead to pursue an education and play college hockey at Boston College, where he enrolled in 1966. Freshmen were not eligible to play varsity hockey at the time, but during the three seasons he did play, Sheehy twice earned All-American honors, scoring 185 points in just 80 games for a point-per-game average of 2.31, a record that still stands at Boston College.

Sheehy then went on to play on U.S. National Teams in 1969, '71, and '72. He was also the co-captain of the 1972 silver medal-winning U.S. Olympic Team as well. After that, Sheehy signed his first professional contract with the New England Whalers of the World Hockey Association. During his eight-year professional career he played for WHA teams in New England, Edmonton and Birmingham, along with NHL teams in Detroit and Hartford. During his pro career Sheehy played in 460 games, scoring 179 goals and 174 assists for 353 total points.

His brother, Neil, who also played in the NHL from 1983-92, with Calgary, Hartford and Washington, is today a Minneapolis-based attorney/hockey agent. Presently, the two brothers work together, signing and representing some of the countries' top hockey talent into the professional ranks.

The Sheehy family, a real class act, remains synonymous with the sport of hockey in International Falls.

THE CLASS OF 1998

Mike "Lefty" Curran

St. Paul Fighting Saints (1973-77)
United States Olympic and National Teams (various throughout 1960s & 70s)

Goaltender

Born: April 14, 1944, International Falls, Minn.

Mike "Lefty" Curran has long been regarded as one of the greatest American goaltenders of all time. Curran achieved success at the high school, college, and Olympic levels. He also starred in the World Hockey Association in the 1970's.

Curran began his illustrious career as an All-State goalie at International Falls, Minn., in the early 1960's, where, in addition to posting a goals against average of 0.78 in the 1961 season — still a Minnesota record, he led his Broncos to a pair of state high school hockey championships.

After playing for a season with the Green Bay Bobcats, of the USHL, Curran decided to attend the University of North Dakota. There the sturdy goaltender led the Sioux to a pair of NCAA Championship games, losing to future Hall of Fame goalie Ken Dryden and Cornell, in 1967, and Keith Magnusson's Denver Pioneers in 1968. The All-WCHA keeper's 2.98 G.A.A. at UND still ranks third on the school's all-time list.

From there he went on to represent the United States seven times in International competition — second only to John Mayasich's nine appearances.

Curran was named as the MVP of the 1972 silver medal winning Olympic Team, in Sapporo, Japan, as his 51-save performance against the Czechs is thought to rival any goaltending performance in Olympic history.

After the Olympics, Curran enjoyed a successful career with the Minnesota Fighting Saints, where, from 1973-77, he stood strong between the pipes. He finally retired from competition in 1977, but not before being named as the Goalie of the 1970s on the USA All-Time Team.

Mike Curran

Bruce Mather

Dartmouth College (1944-48)
United States Olympic Team (1948)
U.S. National Team (1949)

Center

Born: July 25, 1926, Belmont, Mass.

Bruce Mather began his hockey career in Belmont, Mass., where he starred for Belmont High School. Known by the nickname "Little Poison," for his deceptive speed and quick shot, Mather went on to play collegeiately at Dartmouth, in 1943, where he earned a reputation as one of the Ivy League's greatest players of his generation.

Mather centered a line with Ralph Warburton and Bruce Cunliffe which led Dartmouth in scoring for two years. He even led Dartmouth to their infamous 46-game undefeated streak. In 1947 he led the Big Green with 56 points, as the team finished with an outstanding 16-2-2 record, which included a huge win over Michigan, at Ann Arbor that year, sparked by Mather's game-winning goal. And, although there was no NCAA Tourney, Dartmouth claimed the No. 1 ranking in the country that year as well.

In the 1948 Olympics held in St. Moritz, Switzerland, Mather led the United States in scoring and helped the team place fourth in the Games. He was also a member of the 1949 U.S. National Team in the World Championships in Stockholm, Sweden. The highlight for Mather in these Games came in the contest against Austria, when he tallied an impressive five goals in a 9-1 win.

Mather continued his career in the Eastern League with the Boston Olympics, where he was selected "All-League" center. In addition, he was considered one of the best Americans in a predominantly Canadian league. The team regularly played against the likes of Eastern powers such as the New York Rovers, Baltimore and Atlantic City, as well as Canadian powers from the Quebec Senior Leagues too.

After playing for the Boston Olympics, Mather signed with the Boston Bruins in 1950 and later frequently suited-up with the "old time Bruins" for benefit games. In later years, Mather coached various youth teams. Tragically, Mather passed-away suddenly in October, 1975 at the age of 49. He was a true friend to the game of hockey. It was later said that if there was a Lady Byng Trophy (for sportsmanship) for amateur players, he would have won it — hands down.

Joe Mullen

St. Louis Blues (1980-86)
Calgary Flames (1986-90)
Pittsburgh Penguins (1990-95, 1996-97)
Boston Bruins (1995-96)

Wing

Born: February 26, 1957, New York, NY

At the time of his retirement in 1997, Joe Mullen had scored more goals (502) and points (1,063) than any American-born player in NHL history. He earned three Stanley Cups, two Lady Byng Trophies, a Lester Patrick Award and a First Team All-Star berth in his career. He was also inducted into the Hockey Hall of Fame in 2000.

Mullen is a native of New York City and grew up playing roller hockey in the "Hell's Kitchen" section of Manhattan. After playing four years of junior hockey, he went on to play collegeially at Boston College, where he became an All-American in both 1978 and 1979. As a junior, in 1978, he even led the Eagles to the NCAA championship game against rival Boston University.

Following college, Mullen was recruited to be a member of the fabled 1980 U.S. Olympic "Miracle on Ice" team that won the gold medal at Lake Placid. However, because his father was ill at the time, he opted to instead turn pro and use the new income to help out his family. In August of 1979 he signed with the Blues. He was sent down to the CHL for two seasons though, where he proceeded to win both the Rookie of the Year and league MVP awards, respectively.

From there he made the jump to the NHL, where, over the next 15 years he would play with the Blues, Flames, Penguins and Bruins. The speedy and tough goal-scorer was a big fan-favorite wherever he played, and his never-say-die attitude made him a winner both on the ice and off.

Perhaps his most memorable season came in 1989, when he led the Calgary Flames to their first-ever Stanley Cup, and in the process, he was named as a first-team All-Star, received the Lady Byng Trophy (for sportsmanship), and led the league in plus-minus as well. Then, in 1995, he became the first American-born player to ever score 1,000 points in an NHL career.

Fellow United States Hockey Hall of Fame member, the late Bob Johnson, once said of Mullen, when the Penguins acquired him for a second round pick in 1990, "I'd go to war with Joe Mullen."

Mullen retired from the Pittsburgh Penguins in 1997, at the tender young age of 40. In addition, Mullen's brother, Brian, was also in the NHL.

Lou Nanne

Minnesota North Stars (1967-78)

Defense

Born: June 2, 1941, Sault. St. Marie, Ont.

Lou Nanne has one of the most storied careers of any American who has been involved in the game of ice hockey. Aside from being an All-Star player with the North Stars, he was also very involved with the game as an administrator. He served as the team's General Manager for more than a decade, was a member of the International Committee for USA Hockey and also served as Vice President of the NHL Players Association — as a member of the NHL Board of Governors, as a player, coach, GM, and president of the North Stars.

Louie grew up playing Junior hockey with hall of famer's Phil and Tony Esposito. From there he went on to become a member of the University of Minnesota Golden Gopher hockey team from 1959-63, under legendary Coach John Mariucci. There, in 1963, he earned All-American honors in addition to winning the league MVP and the scoring championship.

After graduating from the U of M, he was drafted by the Chicago Blackhawks. But, after a contract dispute, Nanne opted to play for the local Rochester Mustangs of the USHL, while pursuing business interests in the Twin Cities.

Then, in 1968, Nanne served as the captain of the U.S. Olympic Team. (He would also go on to captain of the 1975 and 1977 USA World National teams, while serving as the assistant captain of Team USA in the 1976 1981, 1984 and 1987 Canada Cup tournaments, as well as in the 1994 World Championship.)

After the 1968 Olympics, Nanne joined his hometown expansion North Stars, where he would emerge as the team's first star. Over his 11 year NHL career with the North Stars, including playoffs, he tallied 72 goals and 167 assists for 239 points. From there he became one of the league's shrewdest GM's, running the team until 1990. His 24-year run with the Stars was legendary.

A true friend to the game of hockey, Nanne has received numerous awards and honors, among them being named to the 50 Year WCHA All-Star team, and being awarded the prestigious Lester Patrick Award in 1980 for his outstanding service to hockey in the U.S. Nanne is currently an Executive Vice President for Voyageur Asset Management in Minneapolis. He has become synonymous with game of hockey in Minnesota, and is a real American hero.

THE CLASS OF 1999

Rod Langway

Montreal Canadiens (1978-82)
Washington Capitals (1982-93)

Defenseman

Born: May 3, 1957, Formosa, Taiwan (Raised in Boston, Mass.)

Although from the unlikely birthplace of Taiwan, Rod Langway became one of the NHL's premier defenseman. The six-foot-three, 220 pounder even went on to win the Norris Trophy as the NHL's most outstanding defenseman for both the 1983 and 1984 seasons.

Langway grew up in Randolph, Mass., and attended Randolph High School, where he led the team to a couple of state championship appearances in both 1973 and 1975. From there he decided to attend the University of New Hampshire, where he starred in both hockey and football.

Drafted by Montreal in the second round of the 1977 NHL Entry Draft, as well as by the WHA's Birmingham Bulls, Langway opted to leave school early and play for the Bulls. But, after only one season on Birmingham, he made the jump back to the NHL, where he suited up for the Canadiens in 1978.

There, under the guidance of Hall of Famer Larry Robinson, Langway learned the science of being a defenseman. It didn't take long for the youngster to shine either, as he played a significant role in helping the team to win its fourth straight Stanley Cup title that year.

From there he only got better, even winning a pair of Norris Trophies in both 1983 and 1984, as the league's top defenseman, with the Washington Capitals. The "Stay at Home" defender also went on to captain Team USA at the 1981, 1984 and 1987 Canada Cup tournaments.

All in all, Langway played 15 years in the NHL, earning All-Star honors from 1983-85, and played in six All-Star games as well.

Rod Langway

Gordie Roberts

New England Whalers (1975-79)
Hartford Whalers (1979-81)
Minnesota North Stars (1981-88)
Philadelphia Flyers (1988)
St. Louis Blues (1988-91)
Pittsburgh Penguins (1991-92)
Boston Bruins (1992-94)

Defenseman

Born: October 2, 1957, Detroit, Mich.

Gordie Roberts

Born and raised in Detroit, Gordie Roberts grew up as the youngest of four hockey-loving brothers. So much did his family like hockey, that he was even named after Detroit Red Wing's legend Gordie Howe!

After starring at all youth levels of the game, at the age of 15 he made the jump to play Junior-B hockey for the "Detroit Big D's," which was made up mostly of kids in their late teens. In 1973 he joined the Junior Red Wings of the Southern Ontario Junior League, and quickly got noticed by the professional scouts. By the age of 17 he had signed with the New England Whalers, and well on his way to a long and illustrious pro career.

Known for his rugged style of play and dependability, Gordie Roberts was also an excellent offensive-minded defenseman who could rush the puck up the ice in a hurry. Well liked and respected by his peers, he went on to become a 20-year veteran of professional hockey. The six-foot, 180-pound defenseman was the first U.S. born player to play 1,000 games in the NHL, and also played over 300 games in the World Hockey Association (WHA) for the New England Whalers, totaling over 1,400 combined professional games and registering a combined point total of 606 points. (In addition, Roberts played for Team USA in two World Championship tournaments, and also in the 1984 Canada Cup.)

While he may have gained most of his notoriety in the NHL as a fan-favorite of the North Stars, Roberts was also part of two Stanley Cup Champion teams as a member of the Pittsburgh Penguins in both 1991 and 1992. In fact, Roberts' Pen's beat those very North Stars in the 1991 Stanley Cup Finals.

Over his 15-year NHL career he played for six teams, including: Hartford, Minnesota, Philadelphia, St. Louis, Pittsburgh and Boston. Roberts recorded 10 NHL seasons with 20 or more assists and averaged more than 73 games played as well. He also played in 153 playoff games and scored 57 post-season points as well. In 1993 he also became the first American to play 1000 games in the NHL. He finished his pro career in 1995 while playing in the IHL.

Sid Watson

Bowdoin College

Coach

Born: Andover, Mass., May 4, 1932

A native of Andover, Mass., Sid Watson grew up loving to play hockey. He will he forever linked to Bowdoin College's legendary hockey program, which he oversaw for more than two decades and developed into a four-time ECAC Champion. Watson's hockey teams qualified for the Division II playoffs 16 times and won ECAC Division II championships in 1971, 1975, 1976 and 1978. Overall, he compiled a gaudy record of 326-210-11.

As a hockey coach, Watson has received numerous accolades. He was the recipient of the Eddie Jeremiah Memorial Trophy, recognizing the national Small College Coach of the Year, in 1970, 1971 and 1978; and in 1976 was named as the UPI's Eastern Small College Coach of the Year. In addition, in both 1969 and 1970 he was given the Clark Holder Award as New England's Coach of the Year; and in 1966 he was named as the UPI's New England Coach of the Year. In 1983 he also won the Schaeffer Pen Award for outstanding contributions to New England hockey.

As an administrator, he served as Bowdoin's Athletic Director. He was also the chairman of the NCAA Ice Hockey Rules and Tournament Committee for six years, and served as president, vice president, secretary, treasurer and a member of the board of governors of the American College Hockey Coaches Association. Watson also is a member of the Northeastern University, Maine and Andover, Massachusetts Halls of Fame.

Aside from being a very talented player himself, Watson was also a star National Football League halfback for the Pittsburgh Steelers, from 1955-57, and Washington Redskins in 1958. Over his four-year career in the NFL, Watson rushed for 516 yards and four touchdowns, while adding 423 yards receiving out of the backfield for another two touchdowns. In addition, he was a crafty punt and kick-off return man, even running back another six balls for TDs as well.

Said fellow Hall of Famer, Billy Cleary: "Sid has done so much for the sport of hockey, not only in coaching, but being very active in the AHCA and the NCAA Rules Committee's. He has made tremendous contributions to the sport both as a player, but more significantly as a college coach and administrator. He has developed so many young men as people as well as hockey players."

THE CLASS OF 2000

Neal Broten

Minnesota North Stars & Dallas Stars (1981-95, 1997)
New Jersey Devils (1995-97)
Center
Born: Nov. 29, 1959, Roseau, Minn.

Perhaps nothing says hockey and Minnesota louder than that of Neal Broten. He is without question the Land of 10,000 Lakes' greatest and most beloved player, having seemingly done it all out on the frozen pond.

After leading his Roseau Rams to a pair of high school tournament bids, the speedy forward went on to play an instrumental role as a freshman in leading the Gophers to an NCAA championship in 1979. He notched the winning goal in the Finals against North Dakota and assisted on another which gave him a total of 50 for the year, breaking a 25-year-old school record. He was named WCHA rookie-of-the-year and went on to dominate at the collegiate level.

In 1980, Broten joined Gopher Coach Herb Brooks on the 1980 U.S. Olympic team, where he played a big part in bringing home the gold. From there, he returned to the U of M to play with his younger brother, Aaron, and in 1981, the All-American was named as the first ever recipient of the Hobey Baker Award, honoring the nation's top player.

From there he joined his hometown North Stars, who were in the midst of a playoff run that took them all the way to the Stanley Cup Finals. It would be the beginning of an amazing NHL career, that was later highlighted by another Stanley Cup run in 1991. The North Stars moved to Dallas in 1993, and so did Neal. He was traded to New Jersey in 1995, however, where he finally won a Cup with the Devils.

Fifteen of Broten's 17 years were spent with the North Stars and Dallas Stars, as he closed his illustrious career as the franchise's all time leader in scoring, assists, games played, seasons, shorthanded goals, playoff games and playoff assists. His No. 7 was later retired by the Dallas Stars in 1998.

Neal Broten

Larry Pleau

Montreal Canadiens (1969-72)
New England Whalers (1972-79)

Center

Born: Jan. 29, 1947, Lynn, Mass.

Larry Pleau was named general manager of the St. Louis Blues on June 9, 1997. After two seasons as Blues' GM, Pleau has stabilized the organization's talent base, while steering the team towards challenging for the Stanley Cup.

Under Pleau the Blues have had consecutive first round draft choices, in 1998 & 1999, for the first time in 10 years, and he also introduced player mini-camps for the team's top prospects. His fan and media-friendly approach has gained him respect around the league as one of the most progressive thinking general manager's in hockey today.

In 1999 Pleau signed scoring leader Pavol Demitra to a new contract and re-signed centers Pierre Turgeon and Craig Conroy to new deals as well. He also acquired goaltender Roman Turek from the Dallas Stars prior to the 1999 expansion draft — all moves that led to the team posting the best record in the NHL.

Pleau joined the Blues after spending eight seasons with the New York Rangers organization, most recently as vice president of player personnel. He joined the Rangers in 1989 as assistant general manager of player development.

Prior to joining the Rangers, Pleau spent 17 seasons with the Hartford Whalers organization as a player, assistant coach, head coach, general manager and minor league general manager and head coach. He was also instrumental in drafting Ray Ferraro, Ron Francis, Kevin Dineen and Ulf Samuelsson while a member of the Whalers organization.

Pleau played three seasons with the Montreal Canadiens (1969-1972) in the National Hockey League before being the first player signed by the Hartford Whalers of the World Hockey Association. He was a center/left wing for the Whalers from 1972 until his retirement in 1979. He played in 468 regular season games for Hartford, accumulating 157 goals and 215 assists for 372 points.

In addition, he also played for the 1968 United States Olympic Team, the 1969 U.S. National Team and for Team USA in the 1976 Canada Cup.

One of the game's great innovators, Pleau has emerged as one of the NHL's most successful executives. Larry and his wife, Wendy, have two children: son, Steve, and daughter, Shannon.

Doug Palazzari

St. Louis Blues (1974-82)
Forward
Born: Nov. 3, 1952, Eveleth, Minn.

Doug Palazzari was named executive director of USA Hockey in 1999, signaling yet another important milestone in a lifelong hockey career that has spanned the spectrum from player to coach to administrator.

As executive director of USA Hockey, Palazzari directs the day-to-day operations of a National Governing Body that provides programs and services to more than 560,000 ice and in-line hockey players, coaches, officials and volunteers nationwide.

Prior to being named executive director of USA Hockey, Palazzari oversaw the organization's Youth and Education Programs for eight years, most recently as senior director. His duties provided extensive involvement with the USA Hockey Youth Council, Girls/Women Section and High School Section, as well as supervising the Coaching and Officiating Programs.

As a youngster in Eveleth, Palazzari grew up in a hockey-loving family. His father, Aldo, played for the New York Rangers and Boston Bruins. He went on to star for the Eveleth Golden Bears High School team, and then went on to Colorado College, where he led CC in scoring in both 1972 and 1974, earning All-American and WCHA MVP honors during those same seasons.

Following his college career, Palazzari spent eight seasons (1974-82) playing professionally in the St. Louis Blues' system. He registered 38 points on 18 goals and 20 assists in 108 regular-season games in the NHL, but made his greatest impact while playing for the Salt Lake City Golden Eagles of the CHL — the Blues' top minor league affiliate at the time. Palazzari was twice honored as the CHL's MVP (1978 and 1980) and was tabbed as the league's all-time Greatest Player by The Hockey News as well.

Palazzari's international playing experience includes being selected as a member of the 1973 and 1974 U.S. National Teams, and also representing the United States in the inaugural Canada Cup tournament in 1976.

In addition, he has served in a coaching capacity for USA Hockey several times, most recently in 1991, as head coach for the U.S. Select-16 Team. He was also an assistant for the U.S. at the Olympic Festival in 1991, the 1989 U.S. Select-17 Team and for the teams that represented the U.S. at the 1987 Pravda and 1986 Calgary Cups. He also served as an assistant at CC from 1985-91, as well.

Palazzari, his wife, Sara, and their two sons, reside in Colorado Springs.

THE 1960 U.S. OLYMPIC TEAM

Twenty years before the now infamous "Miracle on Ice" team of 1980, which brought home the gold in Lake Placid, NY, there was another team making history on the other coast of the country, in Squaw Valley, CA. They were the underdog 1960 US men's hockey team who upset some of the biggest hockey powers in the world that February, to give America its first taste of Olympic hockey glory.

The U.S. held its preliminary tryout camps at Williams Arena, on the University of Minnesota campus, under the guidance of the 1956 silver-medal winning Olympic Coach, John Mariucci. After finalizing the roster, the team spent several months playing exhibition games against teams from all over the world.

The Olympic tournament got underway with the Russians and the Canadians being the overwhelming favorites to bring home the gold. The Americans, on the other hand, were not even expected to get past the first couple of rounds. The U.S. came out swinging though, and thanks to five John Mayasich goals, they defeated Australia, 12-1, and Czechoslovakia, 7-5, to advance into the medal rounds. Then, after beating the favored Swedes, 6-3, thanks to Roger Christian's hat trick and his brother Billy's three assists, they went on to beat Germany, 9-1, setting the stage for a showdown with the mighty Canadians. There, behind goalie Jack McCartan's 39 saves, the U.S. beat Team Canada by the final of 2-1.

On February 27th, in front of some 10,000 spectators who had jammed into Blyth Arena, in addition to

The 1960 Olympics Scoring Summary:

Player	Goals	Assists	Points
Bill Cleary	6	6	12
Roger Christian	7	2	9
Bill Christian	2	7	9
Bob Cleary	5	3	8
Paul Johnson	3	2	5
John Mayasich	2	3	5
Tommy Williams	1	4	5
Bob McVey	2	2	4
Jack Kirrane	0	3	3
Weldy Olson	1	0	1
Dick Meredith	0	1	1

The Legendary Brothers' Cleary and Christian

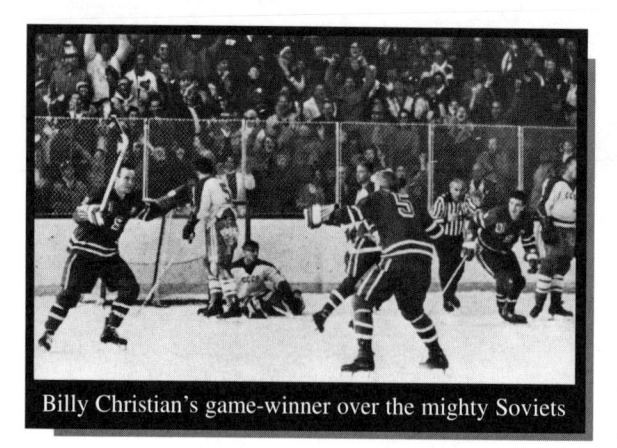

Billy Christian's game-winner over the mighty Soviets

the millions who tuned in on the TV at home, the U.S. team squared off against the Soviet team. Now, this was the era of the Cold War, and there were political ramifications surrounding the game as well, making it all the more dramatic. The game was back and forth, and featured a lot of quick skating and hard hitting. Then, down 2-1 in the second, Billy Christian simply must have decided to take over.

After scoring the game tying goal late in the second, Billy teamed up with his two wing-mates, brother Roger, and Tommy Williams of Duluth, to beat Russian goalie Nikolai Puchkov on a breakaway wrister at 14:59 of the third. McCartan stood on his head for the last couple of minutes, and the U.S. held on to advance to the Gold-medal game against the Czechs.

The US, who had earlier beaten the Czechs, weren't going to take anything for granted. Despite the Americans being noticeably fatigued, they came out strong, and found themselves tied at three apiece after the first period. The squad fell behind, 4-3, after two periods, but then, behind Roger Christian, they

The 1960 Team Roster

Pos.	Name	Hometown	College/Club
G	Jack McCartan	St. Paul, MN	Minnesota
G	Larry Palmer	Wakefield, MN	Army
D	Jack Kirrane	Brookline, MA	None
D	John Mayasich	Eveleth, MN	Minnesota
D	Robert Owen	St. Louis Park, MN	Harvard
D	Rod Paavola	Hancock, MI	None
C	Bob McVey	Hamden, CT	Harvard
C	Paul Johnson	W. St. Paul, MN	Rochester Mustangs
C	Tommy Williams	Duluth, MN	Duluth Swans
W	Dick Rodenhiser	Malden, MA	Boston College
W	Richard Meredith	Minneapolis, MN	Minnesota
W	Weldy Olson	Marquette, MI	Michigan State
W	Bill Cleary	Cambridge, MA	Harvard
W	Bob Cleary	Cambridge, MA	Harvard
W	Roger Christian	Warroad, MN	Warroad Lakers
W	Billy Christian	Warroad, MN	Warroad Lakers
W	Gene Grazia	W. Springfield, MA	Michigan State
Coach	Jack Riley	Boston, MA	Army
Mgr.	James Claypool	Duluth, MN	Duluth
Train	Ben Bertini	Lexington, MA	Lexington, MA

roared back for what would prove to be one of the greatest third periods of Olympic history. Roger struck first at 5:50, followed by Harvard's Bill Cleary, who took a Mayasich pass to put the Americans ahead 5-4. From there, it was all red, white and blue.

Roger added two more goals that final period, to give the U.S. a stunning 9-4 win, and their first Olympic gold medal. Bill Cleary led Team USA in scoring with 12 points, while his brother Bob added eight of his own, and Roger and Billy Christian each added nine points as well.

After the games, the players returned to their respective home-towns as heroes. With that, the game began to grow and expand across the nation. Forty years later the effects of the 1960 team are being felt in places such as California and Florida, where the game has taken off and expanded — not just for our young men, but also for our young women.

It will surely be an exciting time in 2002, when the Winter Olympic Games return to the United States, in Salt Lake City, where emotions will be running high for our Americans — who are now a golden 2-0 in Olympic competition on our own turf. The Hall of Fame proudly recognizes the members of that fabled 1960 team as true American heroes. They should forever be remembered as our nation's first "Miracle on Ice."

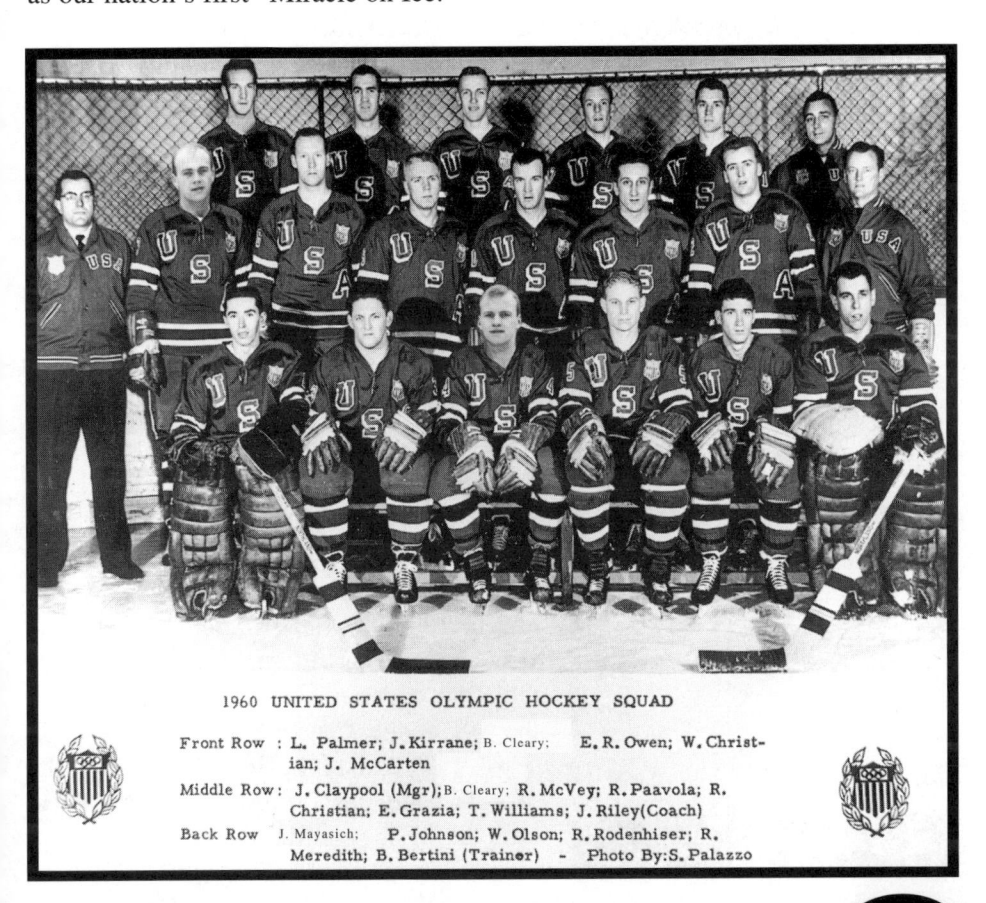

1960 UNITED STATES OLYMPIC HOCKEY SQUAD

Front Row : L. Palmer; J. Kirrane; B. Cleary; E. R. Owen; W. Christian; J. McCarten

Middle Row : J. Claypool (Mgr); B. Cleary; R. McVey; R. Paavola; R. Christian; E. Grazia; T. Williams; J. Riley(Coach)

Back Row   J. Mayasich;   P. Johnson; W. Olson; R. Rodenhiser; R. Meredith; B. Bertini (Trainer) - Photo By:S. Palazzo

THE CLASS OF 2001

Dave Christian

Winnipeg Jets (1979-83), Washington Capitals (1983-90), Boston Bruins (1989-91), St. Louis Blues (1991-92), Chicago Blackhawks (1992-94)
Right Wing
Born: May 12, 1959, Warroad, Minn.

David Christian grew up in a hockey loving family in Warroad, Minnesota. The son of Hall of Famer, Bill Christian, a legendary American amateur hockey star who played with the 1960 gold medal-winning U.S. Olympic team, Dave went on to star at the University of North Dakota, where he tallied 70 points in just 78 games in just two years. From there he went on to play a significant role with the 1980 U.S. Olympic Team, leading the team with eight assists.

The Winnipeg Jets then made Christian their second draft choice in 1979, 40th overall. He stepped right into the NHL with the Jets late in the 1980 season. He made his presence felt immediately, scoring seven seconds into his first shift. He was named captain of the Jets at age 22 and went on to stardom from there. While in Winnipeg during the 1981-82 season, he logged 76 points on 25 goals and 51 assists. Traded to Washington after the 1983-84 season, Christian's best season was an 83-point effort in 1985-86. He went on to put in productive seasons with the Boston Bruins and the St. Louis Blues before ending his NHL career with the Chicago Blackhawks.

He finished his 15 years in the NHL with 340 goals and 433 assists while playing in 1,009 games. Only 151 players, and only 10 Americans, have appeared in more than 1,000 games thus earning him the NHL's coveted Pinnacle Award in 1993. Christian appeared in the Stanley Cup Finals with the Boston Bruins in 1989-90 and in the 1991 All Star Game. His professional days came to an end in 1995-96 after two seasons with the IHL's Minnesota Moose. In addition to his Olympic experience, Christian represented the US at the Canada Cup tournament in 1981, 1984 and 1991. He also played at the World Championships in 1981 and 1989. He currently resides in Moorhead, Minn.

Dave Christian

Paul Johnson

Rochester Mustangs, Minneapolis Millers, Des Moines and Waterloo (1960-72)
Center
Born: May 18, 1935, West St. Paul, Minn.

Paul Johnson grew up playing hockey in West St. Paul, Minnesota. At the age of 21 he was named to the 1958 United States Men's National Team, which competed at the International Ice Hockey Federation World Championship in Oslo, Norway. Johnson was one of just six team members who did not play college hockey.

Before joining the U.S. National Team, he was a member of the Rochester Mustangs, a junior team in Rochester, Minnesota. A dynamic skater and explosive scorer, his appearance at the 1958 IIHF World Championship marked Johnson's first experience with the Amateur Hockey Association of the United States (today known as USA Hockey) and was followed by appearances on two more U.S. National Teams and two U.S. Olympic Teams. This included serving as a member of the 1959 U.S. National Team that competed in the former Czechoslovakia, and the 1961 U.S. National Team that saw action in Switzerland.

In 1960, Johnson was a member of the United States Olympic Ice Hockey Team that captured the gold medal at the VIII Olympic Winter Games in Squaw Valley, California. He scored three goals and added two assists, helping the U.S. to a 5-0-0 overall record. His contributions included the game-winning goal against Canada, the Olympic favorite, on a breakaway.

He was considered by many as the most talented player to come out of Minnesota in that era. Johnson also competed for the U.S. in 1964 at the IX Olympic Winter Games in Innsbruck, Austria. By this time, Johnson had begun a 12-year professional playing career. He spent five seasons (1960-61 through 1965-66) in the IHL, splitting time between the Minneapolis Millers and the Des Moines Oak Leafs. During his time in the IHL, Johnson tallied 218 points on 118 goals and 100 assists in 242 regular-season games. He concluded his playing career in the USHL with the Waterloo Black Hawks. In seven seasons with Waterloo (1965-66 through 1968-69, and 1970-71 through 1972-73), he scored 152 goals and 131 assists, for 283 points.

Johnson and his wife currently reside in West St. Paul, and have 3 children and 2 grandchildren.

Paul Johnson

Mike Ramsey

Buffalo Sabres (1979-93)
Pittsburgh Penguins (1993-94)
Detroit Red Wings (1994-97)

Defenseman

Born: Dec. 3, 1960, Minneapolis, Minn.

Mike Ramsey grew up playing hockey on Minneapolis' many suburban lakes and ponds. After starring at Minneapolis Roosevelt High School, he went on to star as a member of the University of Minnesota's 1979 NCAA Championship team and from there went on to become the youngest player, at just 18, on the fabled 1980 "Miracle on Ice" team. For his efforts he was awarded the Lester Patrick Trophy as a member of the gold medal winning team.

Ramsey went on to play in the National Hockey League for 18 seasons, 14 with the Buffalo Sabres (1979-93), while the next four years were spilt between the Pittsburgh Penguins and the Detroit Red Wings. Ramsey was the Sabres first choice, 11th overall, in the 1979 NHL Entry Draft. Ramsey participated in four (or five) NHL All-Star games in 1982, 1983, 1985 and 1986. He went to the 1995 Stanley Cup finals with Detroit and made a brief two-game comeback during the 1996-97 season before retiring. He holds the Sabres record for most regular season games played by a defenseman with 911. In 1,070 games as a defenseman, Ramsey totaled 79 goals, 266 assists, 345 points and 1,012 penalty minutes. In addition to his Olympic experience, Ramsey represented the United States at the World Championships in 1982. He also played for the American squad at the Canada Cup in 1984 and 1987.

Ramsey returned to the Sabres in 1997 as an assistant coach where he remained until he was named assistant coach of the Minnesota Wild in their inaugural season on July 24, 2000. He helped the Minnesota Wild earn their ranking among the NHL's best in goals against and set an expansion team record in short-handed goals and points in the 2000-2001 season. Ramsey was inducted into the Buffalo Sabres Hall of Fame on February 15, 2001. In addition, Mike currently owns and operates Gold Medal Sports, a popular sporting goods store in Chanhassen, Minn., where he also resides.

IN MEMORY OF STEVEN KIRKPATRICK

The United States Hockey Hall of Fame is proud to recognize the "worlds greatest hockey fan," Steven Kirkpatrick, who tragically died in the Summer of 2001 of cardiac arrest. He was just 22 years old.

Kirkpatrick, who had muscular dystrophy, made history on April 1, 2001, when he became the first wheel chair confined athlete ever to play in a professional hockey game. The Sandusky, Mich., native fulfilled a life-long dream that evening when he signed a one-day contract with the Indianapolis Ice of the Central Hockey League and proceeded to start the game in goal against the Huntsville Tornado.

Amidst the back-drop of thousands of emotional fans, Kirkpatrick came out fully suited up in goalie gear and wearing No. 78, which represented the year he was born. He stood tall for that one glorious shift between the pipes, and even stayed in the action long enough to record a save in the official record book. To make his stint with the team official, Steven signed a one-day contract with the team which amounted to $39. The check, which was prorated from the league's $275 weekly minimum salary, would not get cashed, however, instead becoming framed and mounted on his wall. Commemorating the event were noneother than "Mr. and Mrs. Hockey" themselves, Gordie and Colleen Howe, who had the honor of dropping the puck for the opening face-off to start the game.

In fact, his relationship with the Howe's, Gordie and his wife Colleen, was something very special indeed. The couple had befriended the young man back in 1998, and were instrumental in making the historic game a reality. Since their first meeting, the Howe's invited Kirkpatrick to attend NHL all-star games with them, and he even appeared on a cereal box with them for a charity drive which saw proceeds from the sales going to the Howe Foundation — which assists children with physical and psychological needs. Kirkpatrick also helped start a campaign to build an arena in his native Sandusky, and name it for Colleen. The Howe Foundation even helped purchase a custom van for Steven, so he would have the mobility to not only be an independent person, but also so he would have the ability to see and experience a fuller life.

"Thank God he got to fulfill his dream of playing goalie in a professional hockey game," said Howe. "He will be remembered for his sense of humor and his drive."

Another of Steven's biggest fans was Hall of Fame President, Jim Findley, who later presented the "worlds greatest hockey fan," with a plaque made especially for him by the hall of fame in his honor. Steven even donated some of his game used equipment from his thrilling experience in the crease to the Hall which has now become a new exhibit to honor his memory.

"Anything is possible," said Kirkpatrick, who was diagnosed with Muscular Dystrophy at the age of two. "Even though this disease is tying you down, it doesn't have a full grip on you. I don't have time to sit back and pout about it. If you have a goal, then do it."

A true inspiration, Steven's amazing attitude and positive outlook on life have made him a great ambassador to the game of hockey.

Steven Kirkpatrick

141

IN MEMORY OF SHAWN WALSH

The start of the 2001-02 hockey season was marred by the tragic passing of University of Maine Head Coach, Shawn Walsh. On September 24th, 2001, the 46-year old Walsh finally succumbed to his battle with kidney cancer that he waged so courageously for more than a year.

In 17 seasons at Orono, Walsh led the Black Bears to 399 victories and two NCAA championship titles (1993 and 1999). Four times he was chosen Hockey East Coach of the Year and in 1995, he won the Spencer Penrose Award as the National Coach of the Year.

Walsh coached the U-Maine hockey program to national prominence following his arrival in 1984. His squads won national championships in 1993 and 1999, and made five additional trips to the Frozen Four. He has coached a pair of Hobey Baker recipients in Scott Pellerin (1992) and Paul Kariya (1993), en route to compiling a 399-214-44 (.640) overall record at the school. He ranks 11th among active coaches and 19th all-time in the college ranks with 399 coaching victories.

In addition to team excellence, Walsh's teams produced 28 All-Americans, eight U.S. Olympians, two Canadian Olympians and 35 NHL players. He also produced an 11-0-1 record in international competition. Twice teams that Walsh coached have won the gold medal at the U.S. Olympic Festival (1981, 1990). He also coached the U.S. Select team to victories in 1989 and 1993. Walsh also served as the President the American Hockey Coaches Association from 1993-1995 as well.

Walsh, a native of White Plains N.Y., was born June 21, 1955. He is a 1978 graduate of Bowling Green State University, where he earned both his bachelor's and master's degrees in education. It was also at Bowling Green where he began to concentrate on coaching. In his senior year at the school, Walsh coached the junior varsity hockey team and also worked with legendary head coach Ron Mason at the varsity level. Walsh remained at Bowling Green for two additional seasons with Mason, before the two coaches both moved on to Michigan State.

Prior to Walsh and Mason arriving at MSU in 1979, the Spartans had failed to qualify for the WCHA playoffs in three straight seasons. While at MSU, Walsh helped lead the Spartans to three consecutive CCHA titles and to the NCAA semifinals in 1984, his final year.

From there it was off to Orono, to take over a Black Bear program which, in the three years prior to his arrival was just 27-65-0. Things quickly changed with Walsh behind the bench though, and the rest they say, is history.

Walsh's Black Bears play before standing-room only crowds at Alfond Arena nearly every night and his teams consistently rank among the top 10 in the nation in attendance. His club is traditionally one of the least penalized in the nation and is known for their fast and clean style of play.

A true friend to the game of hockey, Walsh was survived by his Wife, Lynne, and their children, Allie, Tyler, Travis and Sean.

Shawn Walsh

ABOUT THE AUTHOR

Ross Bernstein is the author of several regionally best-selling coffee-table sports books, including: **"Hardwood Heroes: Celebrating a Century of Minnesota Basketball," "Pigskin Pride: Celebrating a Century of Minnesota Football," "Frozen Memories: Celebrating a Century of Minnesota Hockey"** and **"Fifty Years • Fifty Heroes: A Celebration of Minnesota Sports."**

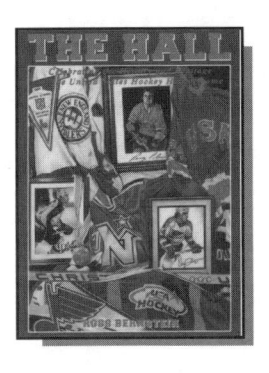

Bernstein first got into writing through some rather unique circumstances. You see, after a failed attempt to make it as a walk-on to the University of Minnesota's Golden Gopher hockey team, he opted to instead become the team's mascot, "Goldy." His humorous accounts as a mischievous rodent, back at old Mariucci Arena, then inspired the 1992 best-seller: **"Gopher Hockey by the Hockey Gopher."** And the rest, they say... is history!

Among Bernstein's other books include several Young-Reader biographies about such sports stars as: Seattle Supersonics Guard **Gary Payton**, Minnesota Vikings Wide Receiver **Randy Moss**, Minnesota Timberwolves Forward **Kevin Garnett** and Vikings Quarterback **Daunte Culpepper**. (Garnett and Culpepper are due out in 2002.)

Today the Fairmont native works as a full-time sports author for several regional and East Coast publishers. In addition, he is also a Contributing Editor and co-founder of a start-up life-style based hockey magazine entitled: **"Minnesota Hockey Journal,"** which has a regional circulation of nearly 50,000 hockey households.

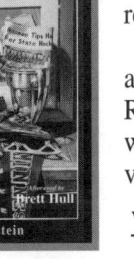

Ross and his wife Sara, along with their sock-snarfing Jack Russell Terrier, "Herbie," presently reside in Oakdale.

To order additional signed and personalized copies of any of Ross' books, please check out his web-site for ordering information or visit your local bookstore. Thanks!

www.bernsteinbooks.com